WRONG NUMBERS

CALL GIRLS, HACKERS, AND THE MOB IN LAS VEGAS

A TRUE CRIME

GLEN MEEK
and DENNIS N. GRIFFIN

WILDBLUE
PRESS

WildBluePress.com

WRONG NUMBERS published by:
WILDBLUE PRESS
P.O. Box 102440
Denver, Colorado 80250

WILDBLUE PRESS is registered at the U.S. Patent and Trademark Offices.

ISBN 978-1-948239-51-6   Trade Paperback
ISBN 978-1-948239-50-9   eBook

Interior Formatting/Book Cover Design by Elijah Toten
www.totencreative.com

WRONG NUMBERS

Table of Contents

DEDICATION

For Shawna and for Max

PREFACE

The city of Las Vegas has had a love/hate relationship with prostitution since the city's inception in 1905. During Las Vegas' incorporation in that year, land adjacent to the railroad tracks was sold to private entities in city block-sized parcels. One of those blocks, in an area off of First Street from Ogden to Stewart, was Block 16, a section designated for saloons that eventually became the city's red-light district.

For years, prostitution, among other vices, flourished in Block 16, and was not merely tolerated, but was, for all practical purposes, officially sanctioned. In those days, a widely held libertarian view in Nevada was that vice in all forms, whether it be gambling, liquor, or prostitution, was best "segregated" in officially recognized areas where it could be controlled and taxed.

After the onset of World War II, however, attitudes in Las Vegas began to change, at least regarding prostitution. Federal intervention in the state contributed to this change of heart, particularly when the US Army established the Las Vegas Aerial Gunnery School to train gunners for military aircraft just north of the city. Many years later, that base would develop into Nellis Air Force Base, which exists to this day.

Military officials in the 1940s did not hide their aversion to brothels near one of their training camps. And by the time the Las Vegas City Commission shut down prostitution in Block 16 in 1942, community sentiment was already moving in that direction. Block 16 was shuttered even before Army officials formally asked for that to happen. However, shortly after the shutdown of Block 16, a brothel established on the outskirts of the city, in an area called the Meadows, was also put out of business, this time directly at the request of the military.

Although city and county officials had laws at their disposal laws which outlawed "public nuisances," there were no state or county ordinances at that time directly banning prostitution. Like a game of whack-a-mole, bordellos would pop up, and when nearby residents objected, officials would bring the hammer down to close them.

In 1954, the federal government once again intervened. Roxie's, perhaps the county's largest and longest operating bordello, was located just outside the city limits, in the cottonwoods off of Boulder Highway about four miles from downtown Las Vegas. In a raid at Roxie's, the feds essentially put an end to the open operation of brothels in Clark County.

The raid targeted the brothel owners, a husband and wife team, for violations of the Mann Act, which outlawed the transportation of women across state lines for prostitution or other immoral purposes. The owners and a manager were all convicted of federal offenses and sentenced to serve between three and five years in prison.

Meanwhile, a crusading Las Vegas newspaper, the *Las Vegas Sun*, put together an undercover sting operation to ferret out corruption connected to Roxie's, with a newspaper contractor posing as a hoodlum seeking to buy Roxie's after the owners were convicted. Political and law enforcement officials were ensnared as they accepted offers of bribes to help re-open the brothel. The undercover operation also revealed connections between some of the corrupt politicians who'd accepted bribes and Mafia figures who held hidden ownership in some casinos.

On January 3, 1955, Roxie's was closed for the last time. It was the last brothel to operate openly in Clark County. In 1971, the Nevada legislature finally took action to regulate prostitution, allowing brothels in rural areas but banning them in counties with a population of more than 200,000 (today that threshold has risen to 700,000), which eliminated Clark County and Las Vegas.

Of course, this did not mark the end of the sex trade in Las Vegas or Clark County, it simply drove the vice deeper underground.

In the post-Roxie's years, prostitutes continued to ply their trade, often in bars, on the streets, or as high-end call girls in the penthouses of some of the new high-rise resorts built in the 1950s and 1960s. But this type of sex-for-sale was much less centralized than the brothel business, and thus less susceptible to organized crime control.

In the 1980s and 1990s, escort services and outcall "entertainment" services began to expand explosively, as the Las Vegas Valley became one of the fastest growing population centers in the country. These services were legal on paper. They offered to send an "escort" to serve as a date or arm candy for a client, or as an "entertainer" whose nominal duty was to perform an exotic dance for a customer.

But police stings showed that in case after case, the vast majority of these escorts or entertainers were really call girls, peddling more than a simple dance or dinner conversation.

Although there were more than 150 of these outcall services licensed in Clark County, Nevada, in the late 1990s, most were owned by only a handful of operators. Once again, sex services were being consolidated into the hands of a few people, but this time the amount of money involved easily dwarfed the revenues of a local brothel. A client of Roxie's might spend $5 for a forty-five-minute fling. A hotel guest in a major strip resort in the 1990s might spend well over $5,000 in a few hours with an escort. And where Roxie's may have employed up to twenty hookers at any given time, there were hundreds, if not thousands, of escorts and outcall entertainers working in Las Vegas.

Once again, organized crime figures began to smell the money. And, according to the FBI, in 1998, a powerful New York crime family made its move to dominate the outcall entertainment and escort industry in Las Vegas.

But few people—especially wiseguys—were aware of how much the oldest profession was being influenced by the newest technology. Today, you can order practically anything over the internet, from Chinese carry-out to an X-rated dancer. But that wasn't the case in 1998.

In the 1990s, the heart of the call girl racket was the phone system. No phone calls—no call girls. No call girls—no call girl racket. It seemed somebody in Las Vegas had found a way to surreptitiously control the calls by electronically diverting phone calls meant for one escort service and redirecting them to a rival service. At least that's the conclusion many escort service owners came to when their call volumes dropped dramatically for no apparent reason.

One of the service owners losing business to the suspected call-stealing scheme took his problem to a New York Mafia associate. That's when, according to federal agents, elements of organized crime hatched a plan to find the call diversion mastermind and put him (or her) under the thumb of a Mafia family.

This development effectively pitted old-school Mob methods against state-of-the-art computer hacking techniques. It would be a race against time for FBI agents to figure out what the suspected wiseguys were up to, who they were targeting, and whether the Las Vegas telephone network—and local outcall service owners—were in danger.

That story is the subject of this book. It's a story we call *Wrong Numbers*.

AUTHOR'S COMMENTARIES

By Dennis N. Griffin

I first became aware of the ongoing prostitution problem in Las Vegas when I was making annual visits there in the late 1980s. Hookers swarmed The Strip, aggressively pursuing tricks—sometimes virtually pulling men away from their wives to have sex—and news racks were loaded with literature advertising escort services. However, I didn't really understand it until 2005 while I was researching for my book *The Battle for Las Vegas*, when I became aware that the world's oldest profession was illegal in Clark County.

I also found a November 3, 1981, article from *The Valley Times* newspaper stating that what I observed was nothing new. The article reported that tourists were unable to walk The Strip without being confronted by the working girls. There had been 15,000 prostitution-related arrests so far that year, with a scant forty-eight convictions. The girls tended to be aggressive and didn't like to take no for an answer. They sometimes physically grabbed onto a male and tried to take him along with them. If he had a female companion with him, she'd be invited to either come and watch or join the action

The district attorney said he couldn't do much with bad arrests and weak cases. The judges argued that they were only able to impose sentences based on the laws currently on the books. Whatever the reasons, prostitution was a major problem in Sin City.

That was interesting to me, but because the primary focus of *Battle* was the Vegas reign and crimes of Chicago Outfit enforcer Tony Spilotro (1971 – 1986), I didn't delve into the prostitution issue any deeper at that time.

In the years since *Battle* was released in 2006, I have given many talks about the Spilotro days and a common question from my audiences is, "After Tony was murdered in 1986, has organized crime left Las Vegas?"

My stock answer has pretty much been, "I doubt it. There's too much money here for them to not want a part of." I wasn't able, however, to be any more specific.

That changed when I was contacted by long-time Las Vegas investigative reporter Glen Meek. I knew of Glen and his work through my nineteen years as a snowbird, splitting my time between central New York and Vegas. I had never personally met him, though. Glen said he was doing a project about the sex trade in Vegas and its connections to organized crime. Would I be interested in participating? *Yes, very much.*

I was in awe of the tremendous amount of material Glen had amassed as we subsequently shared many conversations and correspondence about the topic. The more I learned, the surer I was that I now had an answer to the question about what happened to organized crime in Vegas post-Spilotro.

I think that after reading this book you will be as enlightened and impressed with Glen's work as I have been.

***

By Glen A. Meek

In more than thirty years of covering crime and punishment as a television reporter in Las Vegas, I had an opportunity to report on—and research—almost every kind of criminal enterprise one might imagine, from multi-million-dollar Ponzi schemes to topless bars run like pirate ships. It was natural that organized crime would be a focus of my reporting, given the close connection between the Mob and the casinos in 1980s Las Vegas. During three decades of TV journalism, I chased a lot of wiseguys around the federal courthouse with a camera, trying to capture them on video as they ducked and dodged reporters like me on their way to various court hearings. I covered many scams and shakedowns, murders, and extortion plots. But there was one case that really stood out. And that case is the subject of this book.

This is an organized crime tale that bridges two generations of crooks. It involves allegations of cash in literally obscene amounts, prostitution, the Mafia, and ... computer hackers. That's right: hookers, hoodlums, and hackers.

During a three-decade career of writing about outlaws and illegal activity, this is the only case I encountered where such vastly different criminal cultures collided in such a fascinating manner. On one side: traditional Mob tactics of intimidation and threats of violence. On the other side: a new generation of cyber-crooks who used computers rather than crowbars to hammer their rivals. At stake: control of the huge sums of cash generated by escort services and outcall "entertainment" services, which in most cases were merely thinly disguised call girl operations.

Some of the people caught up in the crime at the heart of this story say they are not wiseguys or Mob soldiers. Certainly, not everyone involved in the caper was a "made man" or a card-carrying (or card-burning, as it were) member of La Cosa Nostra. But the man at the top, the guy giving orders, had very real Mafia ties and some of his "worker bees" spoke openly about being connected to organized crime—when they didn't know they were being secretly recorded by the FBI. There are also other interesting organized crime aspects of this case which you will read about in this book.

Yet, even today, there are lingering questions about the totality of what happened in 1998, when federal investigators allege men, with the backing of a Mafia family, tried to take control of the escort industry in Las Vegas and ran afoul of a technology that traditional hoodlums were ill prepared to deal with. The enduring mysteries surrounding this case keep my interest kindled, more than two decades later, after many of the people involved have served prison terms, retired from law enforcement, died, or simply faded from view.

A quick note on methods and sources: where conversations between the conspirators were captured on court-authorized wiretaps or consensually monitored phone calls, the authors have been able to review transcripts of the calls or listen to actual recordings of the conversations to verify the accuracy of the quotes. Most of the interviews conducted solely for this book were audio or video recorded with permission of the person being interviewed and, therefore, these quotes are essentially verbatim. However, quotes from conversations I had with interviewees and sources back in 1998 are reconstructions based on my own memories, notes, and news stories I wrote at that time. Excerpts from the indictment and search warrant affidavit appear several times throughout this book. The full documents are included in the APPENDIX. Some of the names used in this book have been changed to protect individual privacy.

With that, Dennis Griffin and I hope you will enjoy this book as much as we've enjoyed putting it together for you.

FOREWORD

By Kenny "Kenji" Gallo

I am originally from Orange County, California, where I was with the Milano crime family for many years. I was in a crew headed by Capo/Street Boss Vincent Dominic Caci, better known as Jimmy Caci. Back in those days, we spent a lot of time in Las Vegas due to its proximity to Los Angeles and the many money-making opportunities that thrived in Sin City. That led to my involvement in the lucrative adult escort services that flourished there.

For eight years of my life I wore a wire for the FBI—most of that time was spent in Brooklyn, New York, where I worked among the Colombo crime family—and then this Las Vegas case dropped into my lap.

Twenty years have passed since I helped the FBI in their investigation into the Mafia infiltration of Las Vegas escort businesses. For over a decade I stayed up to date on Mafia news, sharing my thoughts and stories on Breakshot Blog. I gave it up about three years ago, and I no longer keep up with the New York Mafia families' involvements.

And then, a short time ago, I was contacted by investigative reporter and author Glen Meek. He was working on a story about the Chris DeCarlo case, in which the Mafia had helped DeCarlo try to take over the lucrative Las Vegas escort business.

Glen had done his homework. He asked me questions and then filled me in on parts of the story that I did not know. He had researched the case exhaustively, interviewing numerous witnesses, participants, and law enforcement agents. While I had written about my small part in the case in my book *Breakshot: A Life in the Twenty-First Century American Mafia*, I had never been privy to the entire case.

The manuscript Glen sent was so detailed, it drew me right back into the life that I hadn't thought about in recent years but had lived for two decades. It told the story of the old way vs. the new way. It traced the modernization of the world's oldest profession—prostitution—yet revealed that, in the end, it still comes down to plain old-fashioned strong-arm methods.

Escort services generate a lot of cash, and wherever you find dirty cash, the Mafia is sure to be found, too. I remember the first time I heard about Chris DeCarlo, a man who owned escort businesses in Las Vegas. Some Los Angeles gang members told me this crazy tale of a computer whiz who was diverting calls from DeCarlo's escort service and a few others, to their competitors. While the scheme sounded farfetched, I reported it to my FBI handler, who immediately showed a lot of interest. It seems it was very important to the FBI.

The same gang members also mentioned the fact that Gambino family men were sent to Las Vegas to help Chris DeCarlo "deal with the problem." I was under the impression that they would do whatever it took, up to and including murder, to regain their foothold in the escort business.

Chris DeCarlo was never in a Mafia crew, nor had he really lived the street life. I don't think he understood the problems murder would create. The guys who were brought to Las Vegas were no joking matter, they were going to take care of the problem, no matter what.

Glen's book will take you right into the seedy underbelly of Las Vegas. You will get to know the characters and their motivations. The story is still relevant today. Computer hackers, diversion of phone calls, and Mafia heavies, it truly is a modern caper before its time.

I worked with many special agents during the eight years I wore a wire, and while the FBI often gets a bad rap, these men were always top-notch. They worked overtime to keep track of the many players involved in this case. They managed to keep some would-be victims alive in a fluid crime that was moving fast. I remember being on the phone with Chris DeCarlo as the case was going down, FBI agents at my side. Miraculously, no one died or was hurt, due to their competence in the moment.

Hollywood often portrays the Mafia as a group of funny guys who wear suits and crack jokes. The reality is there were no suits in this story, and the only jokes these guys made were about murdering a cohort involved with them in the plot.

Enjoy getting to know the real Mafia in this book. Where did they end up after Las Vegas became a corporate fantasy land? The skimming of the casinos may be over, but the Mafia is an evolving, opportunistic entity that preys on anyone it can exploit.

There really is no honor among thieves.

Chapter One

The Driller Killer

The voice coming over the telephone wiretap was alarming, and the FBI agents listening in knew they would have to act instantly.

"I've got to be quiet," the voice said. "They're in the other room working on some guy."

The voice on the phone belonged to Ken Byrnes, a man the authorities suspected was a Mob troubleshooter sent to Las Vegas from New Jersey to help solve problems plaguing Mob-linked escort services. Byrnes was talking to a Vegas escort service owner who, unknown to Byrnes, was also an FBI informant. Federal agents were monitoring and recording the conversation.

"Vinnie brought his power tools," Byrnes said, then laughed. "I can hear the drill bit going."

"Vinnie" was Vincent Congiusti, an alleged associate of a New York crime family and, according to federal agents, a reputed hitman and torturer. His "power tools" included a cordless drill which he did not bring to Las Vegas to assemble furniture. Word was Vinnie used the drill to bore holes in the heads or kneecaps of guys who wouldn't tell him what he wanted to know. This purported practice would later prompt a tabloid newspaper to dub Vinnie "The Driller Killer."

Vinnie and a couple of other men with alleged Mob ties were in an office complex interrogating a Las Vegas businessman they believed could help them find a mysterious computer programmer. The programmer was thought to be the mastermind behind a phone call diversion scheme that could be costing mob associates millions of dollars. The suspects in this case had been convinced by one of their own that when potential customers called a Mob-linked escort service in Las Vegas, the calls were being electronically intercepted and then redirected to non-Mob affiliated escort operations. Whether the person or persons behind the call stealing scheme knew what kind of people they were messing with was unknown.

Vinnie's job was to make the businessman, who had connections to the escort industry, fork over the location of the person they believed was behind the phone call diversion operation. No doubt the whine of Vinnie's drill would make for a powerful inducement, but there was considerable doubt the businessman actually had the information the suspected wiseguys wanted.

The chilling words coming over the wiretap forced federal agents to make a split-second decision: If they rushed in now, it would mean prematurely ending an ongoing, year-long investigation into organized crime's influence in the Las Vegas escort industry. But, if they didn't raid the office immediately, they feared an innocent businessman might end up with a head resembling a Wiffle ball.

The decision those agents made, and the remarkable facts about the Las Vegas call girl racket that led up to that decision, is the true story behind "Wrong Numbers."

Chapter Two

Visit from a Mom-and-Pop Madam

If the tale you are about to read was a movie idea being pitched by a producer to a studio chief, it might go something like this: imagine "Goodfellas" meets "Risky Business" meets "Wargames."

Somehow, in Las Vegas in the mid-1990s, hired muscle, call girls, computer hackers, and a reputed Mob enforcer who might prefer a Black & Decker to a Smith & Wesson, all became entwined in one of the most unusual organized crime cases in American history. It involved what John Markoff, a writer for the New York Times, would later call "the intersection of the world's oldest profession with the nation's newest technology."

For me, the story started on a spring afternoon with a visit from a nondescript, middle-aged woman who could have been anyone's grandmother. She'd come to see me because at that time I was an investigative reporter for KTNV-TV, the ABC affiliate in Las Vegas.

Turns out, this matronly woman I'll call "Helga" ran a modest "outcall entertainment service." That's essentially an escort service, which, in turn, is generally a polite term for a call girl operation.

Helga had a problem. Somebody was apparently hacking into the telephone system and stealing phone calls to her service. It was as if someone had switched on the call-forwarding feature of her phone without her knowledge or consent.

If a potential customer in a hotel room on the Las Vegas Strip called her service, for example, the call would not arrive at Helga's. Some other escort service would receive it. Her call volume suddenly, and mysteriously, had dropped to practically nothing. And this was especially pronounced when major prize fights or other sporting events took place in Las Vegas, traditionally big weekends for the escort businesses.

Naturally, I asked Helga why she didn't go to the police, since escort and outcall entertainment services were licensed establishments—legitimate as long as they stuck to actually escorting visitors and performing exotic dances.

"You know the police don't believe the services are legit," she said. "They have absolutely no sympathy for anything that impacts our business."

Her point was well taken. Las Vegas Metro police had been claiming for years the outcall services were nothing but fronts for prostitution. Their investigations confirmed this, as in undercover sting after undercover sting, when officers posing as customers called escorts or outcall "dancers" to hotel rooms, virtually every woman who showed up offered sex for money.

From a financial standpoint, the outcall services almost had to be involved in prostitution (which is legal in rural Nevada, but not in Clark County where Las Vegas is located) because no male visitor was likely to call a woman to his room and pay the prices the women were asking just to watch a private dance.

"I'd be surprised if five percent of these girls even know how to dance, I mean in anything resembling a professional manner," laughs Jack Sheehan, author of *Skin City*, a book about the sex industry in Las Vegas. "No guy who calls an escort service and has a girl come to his room wants the evening to end with a nude dance. Let's be real."

So, there was little debate about what was really going on with the vast majority of escort services. And I wanted to know from Helga why she thought TV news viewers would be interested in a story about an industry many believed was a shady and barely legal front for illegal prostitution.

"Because it's not just about outcall," she said. "Right now, they're targeting us because they figure we're not likely to complain to the cops. But what happens when this spreads to other, one hundred percent legitimate businesses, like pizza delivery places or cab companies?"

Her question was intriguing, and I was absolutely interested in any criminal conduct that might affect the integrity of the phone system.

But I wanted proof it was actually happening.

"Come to my office later this afternoon," Helga said. "I'll show you some proof."

Her "office" was in an industrial strip mall off of Valley View Boulevard, only a few blocks north of the TV station. It had a roll-up garage door and was the kind of place used by moped rental dealers and small engine repair shops. I admit I had some trepidation about going there alone, as she'd insisted. But I left word at the TV station where I'd be should anything happen.

There was no signage on the place and the door had a speakeasy-style slot where the people inside could see a visitor before granting them admission. When I knocked, Helga let me in.

The office was furnished in Early Garage Sale: an old desk, a PBX phone, and some telephone call logs on the desk surrounding the phone.

Helga pulled out a sheet of paper from the desk, a hotel "folio," or billing sheet, that showed charges rung up on a room. She said it had been given to her by a man who came to her office with a complaint about one of her escorts.

The folio was from a major strip resort, one of the hotels that charged for local phone calls. One of the numbers Helga used in ads for her service (most services used multiple numbers) was printed on the folio, indicating the customer had called one of Helga's lines. But Helga showed me her call logs for that night and there was no customer who phoned from that hotel on that evening and she sent no escort there.

Helga went on to explain that the hotel guest was upset because the escort who came to his room "rolled" him. He had reported that while he was taking a shower, at the escort's request, the escort swiped his cash and a Rolex watch before any business between them was conducted. He'd gotten screwed, but only metaphorically.

Fortunately, when the disgruntled hotel guest came to see Helga, her driver was in the office with her. The driver was a large young man who also sometimes shuttled the escorts to the various hotels to meet their clients and served as a quasi-bodyguard. The hotel guest was angry and didn't believe Helga when she told him she never sent a woman to his room, that somehow his call had been diverted to another service and that other service was responsible for him being rolled.

The presence of Helga's driver may have kept the hotel guest from doing anything rash, and the unlucky man was not in a position to go to the cops, what with him being a family man in town on business without his wife. The guest left, but also left behind his hotel folio with the number for Helga's service on it.

Helga's story, and the folio from the strip hotel impressed me. Certainly, Helga could have made all this up and possibly forged the documents—but what would be her motive? She certainly didn't want to call more attention to her business than she needed to.

Before committing to put a story on the air, I wanted to run it by two sources; one in the adult entertainment industry, the other a high-ranking Las Vegas FBI agent.

First, I called the adult entertainment source, a guy named Eddie Munoz, who owned most of the news racks on The Strip. The number and placement of news racks on The Strip was tightly controlled by the county commission, and they were not being used to vend *The New York Times* or *The Wall Street Journal*. These news racks were filled with pamphlets advertising escorts and outcall "dancers." The headlines for these publications read something like "Blond Asian MILFs want to meet you tonight!" and generally featured pictures of scantily clad women, although there were a few that also depicted nearly naked men.

Eddie had a license as an outcall entertainment promoter as well as owning news racks. When I got him on the phone, I couldn't get him to stop talking. He not only confirmed that the same thing that was happening to Helga was happening to him, but said other outcall service owners were also reporting a sudden drop in call volume during peak hours. Eddie was actually contemplating a lawsuit against the phone company.

"My phones were ringing fine," Eddie told me in an interview, years later. "I was doing about a hundred calls a day. All of a sudden, it just tapered down to about fifty percent.

"I just thought, 'Oh, business is down.' Then it went down lower than that. And then it went to nothing.

"I knew from being in the business since I was sixteen years old, something was wrong."

The fact that Eddie and others were also having trouble made the call diversion story more plausible to me; if someone was going to hack the phones of competitors, you'd want to include more than just mom-and-pop operations like Helga's.

Also, my conversation with Eddie and others told me that the larger outcall operations seemed to be doing just fine even though the smaller companies were losing business. Although it's possible the larger escort services might simply be weathering a downturn in business better than the little guys because of their size, the mom-and-pop operators were convinced the big guys were still doing big business because whoever was stealing the phone calls was doing it for the top three or four escort service owners.

The complaints from Eddie and Helga prompted me to arrange a meeting with my FBI acquaintance for breakfast at a popular West Sahara Avenue eatery. I wanted to let the agent know what I'd been told, see if the Bureau was aware of the call-stealing allegations and, if so, find out what the FBI was doing about it.

The senior agent kept a poker face all through his huevos rancheros.

"Glen, as you know, prostitution is basically a local crime and, at that, a misdemeanor in Las Vegas," the agent said. "The Bureau doesn't normally get involved unless there's an element of human trafficking involved or some other crime that crosses state lines."

"But we are also interested in other crimes that might be associated with prostitution, like money laundering, extortion, and shakedowns. We always want to know more about that kind of thing. And, obviously, the security of the phone system is high on our list. I can tell you this: if something we're working on leads to an indictment, you'll get the first call."

Now, we were getting somewhere. It seemed clear he was telling me—without telling me—that the Bureau was working on something involving the outcall industry. He wasn't going to confirm it, or tell me the nature of the investigation, but at least I'd been assured I'd get the first call if arrests were made.

I paid for breakfast and thanked the agent for his time. Not long after that, I aired a story about the alleged call diversion, interviewing Helga in silhouette and disguising her voice. The story raised a few eyebrows but didn't make any waves.

A year later, when I'd almost forgotten about it, I got that phone call that had been promised.

Indictments had been unsealed, and the allegations were startling. They involved the Gambino La Cosa Nostra (LCN) family of New York, a plot to take over the outcall industry in Las Vegas, a shadowy computer expert some believed was behind the call diversion, and an alleged "made man" with the Mafia whose moniker reflected his mission to eliminate the Mob's headaches: Vinnie "Aspirins" Congiusti.

Chapter Three

Welcome to Las Vegas

At the south end of the Las Vegas Strip stands perhaps the most iconic neon sign in America. Designed by Betty Willis in 1959 for the Western Neon company, the sign is a rounded diamond shape with a row of seven circles on top, each circle representing a silver dollar. Twenty-four hours a day the sign flashes a solitary message: Welcome to Fabulous Las Vegas, Nevada.

In recent years, the sign has become such a popular attraction that the Clark County Commission actually created a mini park around it, to allow visitors to park their cars and pose for pictures with the sign.

Anthony Nastasi's welcome to Las Vegas was anything but fabulous and did not involve the iconic sign on the south end of The Strip. It did, however, end with him having his picture taken: a mug shot.

Nastasi was a tough, forty-something, silver-haired New Yorker who had taken over an escort service in The Big Apple after the owner couldn't pay a debt. In the late 1990s, Nastasi saw the potential for expanding his business into the Las Vegas market, where the local phone book was packed with more than one hundred full page ads for escorts or, as they were commonly called, outcall entertainment services.

Being an escort operator from New York and of Italian extraction, Nastasi was no stranger to wiseguys. He rubbed elbows with people in the Mafia, had his own Mob connections, and, from time to time, had helped the FBI with investigations into organized crime. Nastasi likely knew Las Vegas was an open city. No single Mafia family reigned over the illegitimate or even semi-legitimate activities there. Any crime family could operate in Las Vegas without paying a street tax to any other family. Nastasi might have anticipated that he would be contacted by local wiseguys, or connected guys, once he set up shop in Las Vegas. They may offer their "family connections" to help him avoid hassles with local cops or licensing officials in exchange for a small piece of his action.

He may have expected, in short, to be the target of a shakedown at some point. But when it happened, even this hardened Mob associate was shocked by the gang that did it. That gang, Nastasi claims, was the Las Vegas Metropolitan Police Department.

Not long after he'd put together an escort operation in Las Vegas, Nastasi went to the Desert Inn Hotel and Casino to meet a madam from California. The madam had clients in Hollywood and elsewhere in southern California who were celebrities or corporate big shots, and those high rollers frequently found themselves in Las Vegas. The madam wanted to work out an arrangement where she would refer her clients to Nastasi's operation when they were in Vegas, and Nastasi would then kick-back some of his profits to the madam.

While waiting for the madam to show, Nastasi decided to pump a few dollars into a slot machine. He had run the machine up to a nearly $500 payout when he felt a tap on his shoulder. It wasn't the madam.

"I turn around, and there he is with his little star," Nastasi remembered in a radio interview with Las Vegas newsman George Knapp for the program *Coast-to-Coast AM*.

"And I said, 'Yeah, who are you, The Lone Ranger?'"

The man who'd tapped Nastasi on the shoulder was neither alone nor a ranger, but his star was a real badge and he was an undercover vice officer from Las Vegas Metro Police, better known as Metro. The vice cop had a few plain-clothed brother officers with him, and they busted Nastasi for pandering.

Outside the Desert Inn, the officers pushed the handcuffed Nastasi into the back seat of a Camaro that had apparently been confiscated by police in a previous case and converted into an undercover cop car. The driver, a different officer from the one who tapped him on the shoulder, tried to engage Nastasi in conversation. Among other things, Nastasi said, the vice cop mentioned that he was from Ozone Park in New York, the former territory of Gambino family crime boss John Gotti.

"And he was trying to relate to me," Nastasi said in his radio interview. "He says, 'You know how things are done, and I know how things are done. We're entitled to a little taste.'"

Nastasi claims he replied, "You're entitled to a taste of what? What do you mean, you want me to buy you a pizza or something? What are you talking about?"

Nastasi knew full well what the officer was allegedly talking about: protection money, a little piece of Nastasi's action to keep the cops out of his hair. But Nastasi said he feigned ignorance to draw the officer out.

The officer, according to Nastasi in the radio interview, finally put it bluntly. "You wanna do business in this town, you know, you do business with us," the vice cop allegedly said. "And everything is fine, we make everything go away and everything is fine."

At this point Nastasi said he told the undercover cops that if they wanted to be partners with him, they'd have to put up some money. That seemed to chill the conversation down to a much cooler temperature, say absolute zero. The officers, according to Nastasi, never brought up the subject of paying for protection again.

But when they got to the jail, Nastasi said, one Metro officer did have a nonverbal message for him when he asked for help getting out of the confined seating of the Camaro because his hands were cuffed behind his back.

Again, from the *Coast-to-Coast AM* interview:

"I told the guy, do you wanna give me a hand getting out?" Nastasi said. "And he says, 'Sure,' and he throws me to the floor. And he goes to work on me with his pointy cowboy boots."

Nastasi said the officer kicked him multiple times while he was on the floor, but the New York Mob associate claims he only chided the cop for being weak, saying, "Do all cops kick like little girls?"

That, Nastasi said, earned him a few more kicks. Soon after, he was booked into a holding cell with what he calculated were ninety other guys in a room designed to hold maybe twenty. He figures he was behind bars for forty-four hours before his lawyer finally arranged for bail and got him out.

Though Nastasi said he had plenty of friends and associates in organized crime, he knew he could not go to any Mob pals for help with what had just happened. As he told George Knapp:

"Wiseguys can only protect you from their own kind. You tell them you got a problem with cops shaking you down, and they're gonna run into the woods like little squirrels. They don't want no part of that and they ain't gonna wanna hear it."

So, after he got out of the Clark County Detention Center, Nastasi called one of his FBI contacts in New York, who put him in touch with federal agents in Las Vegas.

Nastasi's introduction to the Las Vegas FBI agents was a godsend for the feds. The Las Vegas FBI office had been following the explosive growth of the outcall entertainment, or escort, industry. The 130-150 full page ads for escorts in the phone book told much of the story: each full-page ad cost roughly $3,000 dollars a month. So, the organized part of the escort industry was spending roughly half a million dollars a month just for phone book ads. If the advertising budget for a single medium was nearly half a million dollars a month (and don't forget there were also The Strip news racks and handbillers who dispensed pamphlets on the street advertising the services), that suggested the services themselves were generating many millions of dollars a year.

But up until this point, the feds had been unable to penetrate the outcall agencies. They had no one on the inside. With Nastasi, that was about to change. Nastasi not only told agents he would act as their informant; he would allow an actual FBI agent to work undercover as a manager in his escort service.

This is how Special Agent Charles Maurer, who would oversee the escort investigation for the FBI with fellow Agent Jerry Hanford, described the undercover operation in an affidavit for a search warrant:

> *This investigation was predicated upon information received from numerous sources which indicate that a significant portion of the outcall business in Las Vegas, also known as the escort service business, is merely a front for money laundering, robbery, prostitution, narcotics distribution, and other criminal activity.*
>
> *Previous investigations of the outcall business by the FBI and local law enforcement have focused primarily on the act of prostitution rather than on the individuals who operate the business. These investigations have had little success because those outcall service operators who operate illegally shield*

themselves from prosecution by claims of ignorance as to the prostitution and other illegal activities. In addition, investigations focusing on prostitution have little jury appeal because prostitution is legal in many areas of Nevada, although not in Las Vegas.

Consequently, a decision was made to initiate an undercover operation (UCO) which would target not prostitution, but those crimes traditionally associated with the LCN such as extortion, murder, and money laundering.

Special Agent Mauer is now retired, but when the FBI began its outcall investigation in late 1997, Maurer was well aware, from his own personal experience, how easily greed and organized crime could combine to make a murder. He'd already seen evidence that Mob associates were nibbling at the edges of the Las Vegas escort industry.

Only a year prior, in 1996, Mauer had been working undercover as part of "Operation Thin Crust," an FBI operation to infiltrate a group of wiseguys from several different mobs who'd formed a loose alliance in Las Vegas. The crooks were associated with crime families in L.A., New York City, and Buffalo. Maurer, in his guise as Charlie Moreno, an alleged burglar and check forger from Cleveland, was able to get inside this group, which had ties to Herbie Blitzstein. Blitzstein had been the right-hand man of Tony Spilotro, considered by law enforcement to be the Chicago Outfit's chief enforcer in Las Vegas in the 1980s. Spilotro was killed in 1986, during a trip home to Chicago, and his badly beaten body was found in an Indiana cornfield. Spilotro was the gangster portrayed by Joe Pesci in the movie *Casino*.

Spilotro's former associate Herbie Blitzstein was one of the few Mob guys from that era who was still making a good living in Vegas in the 1990s, primarily from high-interest juice loans he had on the street. Blitzstein had also taken at least $10,000 in protection money recently from an outcall entertainment service owner. The "protection" provided by the wiseguys amounted to the gangsters agreeing not to harass or intimidate the service owner's handbillers, who handed out pamphlets on The Strip promoting the escort services. Those handbillers were often undocumented immigrants who were paid minimum wage and were highly susceptible to threats.

But when the outcall service owner refused to make any additional protection payments, a couple of goons connected to Blitzstein tried to shake down the agency owner at a local steakhouse. That led to fisticuffs between the outcall business owner and the Mob guys and prompted the restaurant management to call the cops. Although several wiseguys were involved in the beef at the steakhouse, only one, an L.A. Mafia associate, was charged in the case. His name was Johnny Branco.

When it came time for the outcall service owner who was extorted and roughed up to testify against Branco, the victim was a no-show and the charges against Branco were dropped. Branco walked out of court a free man. However, the lack of support he received from his fellow wiseguys while facing the charges would later enter into his decision to become a federal informant.

As for Blitzstein, less than a year after the incident at the steakhouse, the graying Mob associate was robbed and murdered in his own home by some of the other wiseguys he'd been doing business with (though not Branco). The killers were in, or connected to, the same crew that Agent Maurer had infiltrated, and they were soon rounded up and jailed. Mauer now had a recent up-close-and-personal reminder of how quickly wiseguys could turn on each other where even a whiff of cash was involved. The incident at the steakhouse further demonstrated that Mob guys were already trying to muscle money out of the local escort industry.

So, in November of 1997, with the aid of a New York Mob associate, the Federal Bureau of Investigation— in a manner of speaking—became silent partners in Tony Nastasi's Las Vegas escort service as part of a long-term undercover operation. It was not long before guys with organized crime connections came calling, and an astonishing allegation about the industry surfaced: that someone had developed a "black box" electronic device that could steal phone calls meant for one service, and re-route them to another.

To the Mafiosi, this could mean millions of dollars in business they weren't getting that somebody else was. According to investigators, the word went out to Mob enforcers to find whoever was behind that black box and make them an offer they couldn't refuse: use your call diversion device to help us get a bigger piece of the escort racket or find yourself planted like a yucca bush in a remote part of the Mojave Desert.

Chapter Four

All About Outcall

The late 1990s were the golden years for outcall entertainment, or escort, businesses in Las Vegas. Legal on paper, the services were licensed by the city and county for the purpose of providing "entertainers" who could be called by customers to perform an erotic dance, in either the customer's hotel room or, if the customer was a local, their home. But the reality of the situation was that these services were primarily a method for prostitutes to connect with johns. The outcall services were part of the latest, and possibly most efficient, evolution of the world's oldest profession.

Prostitution has been legal in Nevada since before statehood, and Nevada is the only state in the union where it is legal today. However, it's only permitted in rural areas of Nevada, and not in Washoe County, where Reno is located, nor in Clark County, where Las Vegas sits. But, because Las Vegas is the most populous city in Nevada and a tourist Mecca as well, the demand there for sex workers is significant.

Although Las Vegas shut down its red-light districts in 1942, it wasn't until 1971 that the Nevada legislature took action to regulate prostitution in the state, when the state legislature enacted a law permitting prostitution only in licensed brothels, and then restricted brothels to counties with populations of less than 200,000 (later 700,000). That excluded Clark County and, thus, Las Vegas.

"Nevada's had this weird relationship with the sex industry," said Michael Green, history professor at the University of Nevada Las Vegas. "Nevada tolerates it, often encourages it—and then says, 'Oh, we want nothing to do with it.'"

Despite the official ban in Clark County, illegal prostitution flourished in Las Vegas, where working girls trolled the casino bars seeking customers or cultivated hotel bellmen, desk clerks, and valets to act as procurers. It was an old-school system, and a potentially dangerous way for hookers to hook up with clients. The sex worker never really knew what kind of guy she was picking up, and the guy seeking sex never knew if the woman he was hiring was working for a violent pimp who would help her roll the customer.

The outcall entertainment business model revolutionized the sex industry in Las Vegas. Because the "entertainers" had to be registered and obtain a work card with the county (they were supposed to, anyway), it tended to keep women (and men, but there were far fewer of them) with previous prostitution convictions or serious police records out of the business. That gave the industry a veneer of legitimacy, which instilled confidence in the customers. Most johns would rather call a phone number from a Yellow Page ad or pamphlet they pulled from a news rack on The Strip, which seemed to resemble a legitimate business, than cruise down a dark side street looking for action and wondering if that streetwalker had a gun in her purse. Or, perhaps a gun and a badge.

For many prostitutes, the outcall entertainment formula was a significant improvement over the old pimp-and-ho system. A number of women, for the first time, were able to work without pimps.

Make no mistake: many pimps did force women under their control to sign up with these services, at least those who were able to obtain a work card. And, certainly, there was sex trafficking in the industry. But the outcall system also allowed a number of women to decide for themselves whether or not to work as a prostitute. They could sign up with several agencies if they chose to and work as little or as much as they wanted. It gave rise to a system of sex workers as independent contractors, although the agencies took a lot of money off the top while the entertainers did the majority of the grunt work.

The outcall entertainment services were largely an outgrowth of the escort industry, and the two kinds of adult businesses are virtually interchangeable. However, owners of outcall "entertainment" services may be more apt to claim a constitutional protection for their businesses since erotic dancing has been ruled by various courts to be an art form protected by the First Amendment. Of course, if that "dancing" is nothing more than the proverbial horizontal bop, then it's just another front for prostitution like many (if not most) escort services.

The huge sums of cash generated by these escort services made for strange bedfellows. Entire cottage industries developed to support the growing outcall empire. There were publishing companies that catered almost exclusively to the escort services, producing the pamphlets promoting outcall entertainers found in news racks or handed out in person by pamphleteers or handbillers on The Strip. The Yellow Pages, where families might look up the phone number of a local pizza parlor or where you might go to find a dentist with an office near your house, became the chief advertising arm for an army of hookers posing as hoofers. Money was flowing from outcall, and a lot of birds were dipping their beaks in the stream. Yellow Pages account executives, word was, suddenly started shopping for beachfront vacation homes.

The phone book ads for outcall services became so numerous, and so lurid, that people began to joke that the slogan "Let your fingers do the walking" referred to streetwalking.

Since phone books containing the Yellow Pages were in practically every home in Las Vegas in those days, families with children started insisting that Clark County politicians do something about the ads. The politicians, in turn, put pressure on the Yellow Page people and restrictions were ultimately placed on the types of artwork permitted. Photographs and depictions of actual people were no longer allowed, though the ads themselves were not banned from the Yellow Pages. The ads ended up featuring clean-but-sexually-suggestive imagery like lingerie hanging over a chair, pearl necklaces, half-empty cocktail glasses with a bedpost in the background and—literally—hearts and flowers.

But those restrictions only impacted the phone book. The pamphlets handed out on The Strip or dispensed from news racks continued to feature barely dressed women.

You might have looked at one of those outcall advertisements in the 1990s and wondered why some of the women (usually it was a woman) shown in the ad would be involved in the escort trade. "They're beautiful," you might say. "They should be models."

And, of course, they *were* models. Their pictures had simply been pirated from the newly created online editions of *Playboy* and *Penthouse* magazines. That led to an early skirmish in the battle over intellectual property rights on the internet that continues to this day.

I put together a television news story about this after a top security officer for Playboy Enterprises called and asked me to lunch. He'd seen some of my previous television stories about the friction between the outcall industry and local law enforcement and was looking for any information I had about the publishing companies that promoted the escort services. I pointed him to a recent lawsuit that some of the handbill publishers had joined against the county, which was trying to curb the amount of escort service advertising being handed out on The Strip. In the lawsuit, the publications self-identified as being connected to the outcall industry.

The security chief explained to me that on a recent visit to Las Vegas, *Playboy* publisher Hugh Hefner was with an entourage of guests when he was handed an outcall promotional flyer that depicted his then-wife, Kimberly Conrad, as an escort.

"What we want to do," the *Playboy* executive told me, "Is sue the shit out of some of these people and make them stop pirating our pictures."

"There is so much stuff out there in the public domain, that there's no reason to use photos that are proprietary," said Allen Lichtenstein, a former lawyer for the ACLU who worked on behalf of Las Vegas escort services on First Amendment issues. "And I think that's what they figured out."

Lichtenstein said he always advised his clients not to use anyone else's photos to depict entertainers. However, he did push back when Clark County officials suggested that the mere use of non-escort, professional models to depict outcall "entertainers" was evidence that the outcall entertainment companies were not legitimate. Lichtenstein's answer to county regulators:

"When you go to the Chevy dealer to get your car repaired, you don't really get Mr. Goodwrench."

All these years later, it's difficult to determine if *Playboy* ever filed any lawsuits over photo piracy. Perhaps cease and desist letters did the trick. In any event, the outcall pamphlet publishers stopped using copyrighted photos (at least those from *Playboy*). Even today, many of these publications carry the disclaimer "Photo seen is that of actual entertainer!"

Another news story I aired around the time of the models-versus-actual-escorts controversy illustrates just how unbridled the escort industry in Las Vegas was in the 1990s, with few fast rules and a lot of people applying questionable, situational ethics to their business practices.

In the mid-to-late 1990s, print was still king when it came to advertising escort services, and with the Yellow Page ads being toned-down, the more titillating publications dispensed on The Strip took on greater importance for the outcall industry.

Many of the flyers and handbills passed out on The Strip still showed nearly naked or topless women, often with only photoshopped "stars" covering their nipples or pubic areas.

Here again, Lichtenstein counseled his outcall service clients to go easy; ads that left little to the imagination just weren't necessary, he said, considering the nature of the services being advertised.

"I always told my clients, look, you don't need to go anywhere near that line. Anyone who's looking for what you're offering is gonna understand it. It's kind of pointless to fight over that."

But the lawyer's advice was not always followed.

Along with the handbillers, news racks continued to dispense some of the more ribald advertising for outcall services. These news racks, which dispensed free promotional material for escort services, were closely regulated by the county in terms of how many were allowed on The Strip at any time, and where they could be located. For example, there might be ten news rack locations on The Strip and each location may allow only six news racks. These news racks had permits affixed to them by the county to show they were properly licensed.

But for a time, every night just after dark, once the county inspectors knocked off for the day, groups of men in U-Haul trucks would cruise down The Strip unloading illegal news racks in the same locations where the ones with permits were sitting. The outlaw news racks, like the "legit" ones, were stuffed with outcall promotional handbills, but had no permits from the county.

Then, in the early morning hours before the county inspectors came back on duty, the same men in U-Hauls would collect the illegal news racks. It happened night after night for months before county regulators got wise and started working their inspectors in shifts, confiscating the unpermitted news racks and impounding them. The owners could come collect them and pay a fine, but few, if any, did. It was better to not identify yourself as a news rack pirate, and the cost of a brand new news rack was about the same as the fine.

Although county inspectors eventually cracked down on the outlaw news racks, Eddie Munoz, who operated an outcall service as well as owning properly permitted news racks, said all too often local law enforcement paid little attention to the problems of the adult entertainment industry.

"They usually let us fight our own battles, and we had wars out there on the street," Munoz said.

Attorney Lichtenstein believes police, politicians, and even the owners of strip resorts were less worried about acts of prostitution connected with the outcall services than they were about the overt and open advertising. This was particularly true regarding the pamphleteers and handbillers who handed out flyers on the street. Resort officials were getting a steady stream of gripes from tourists about the handbillers, who they complained were thrusting salacious, adult-oriented material at them as they strolled up and down The Strip with the wife and kids. This was happening even as Las Vegas started developing (erroneously, it turned out) a reputation as becoming a more "family-oriented" destination.

"What they were concerned about with the handbillers, was the visibility," said Lichtenstein.

And while some police administrators viewed the outcall services themselves as being a low-level form of organized crime, up until this point involvement by the actual La Cosa Nostra had been limited to a few incidents like the extortion of the outcall service owner mentioned earlier in this book. Nonetheless, a quasi-legal industry generating millions of dollars in cash while police and politicians seemed powerless to stop it, would constitute an engraved invitation to Mob bosses looking to make money in a town that had recently run them out of the casino industry.

"Outcall services, prostitution, topless clubs—these are operations that run on cash," said UNLV's Michael Green. "So, if the Gambino (crime) family has people with brains, and they certainly did, they're gonna look at Las Vegas and say, okay, it's hard to get into the casinos and we want to make money. Where do we make it?"

Many people have the impression that the Mob "ran" Las Vegas, at least until the mid-1980s, and therefore controlled prostitution in the city. The scene in *The Godfather, Part II* where a Nevada senator gets compromised during a fatal encounter with a hooker in a Mafia-controlled brothel probably contributes to that notion.

The fictional senator, Pat Geary, was loosely based on the real Senator Pat McCarran. McCarran was rumored to have been a behind-the-scenes political protector of a Clark County brothel called Roxie's, but that allegation was never proved. Roxie's closed in 1955, following a federal raid. Some of the people involved with Roxie's were later revealed to have links to mobsters who also held hidden interests in local casinos. Senator McCarran was not one of them.

But Las Vegas has always been an open city as far as organized crime is concerned, and no single crime family had control over prostitution or any other vice. Individual mobsters or wiseguys might be running a "stable" of hookers or call girls, but no single person or family was in overall charge of the sex trade. Also, prostitution had largely been decentralized following the closure of the brothels in Clark County.

The rise of the outcall services changed that to a great extent. Because of outcall agencies, sex work became organized, commercialized, and, in a very real sense, industrialized. Some of these services operated like factories, and if the workers couldn't keep up, or grew tired of the grind, they were often replaced with newer models. Young, starry-eyed women (and a few men) looking to make big bucks with little formal education were the grist for some of these sex mills.

In a thesis for her master's degree at the University of Nevada Las Vegas, on the topic of labor violations in the outcall industry, Candice Michelle Seppa Arroyo describes working for a time in 2001 as a "phone girl" for Sweethearts and for Playmates, pseudonyms for two of the top Vegas outcall outfits. The job of a phone girl was to answer phone calls to the agency and book dates between customers and the "dancers" or "entertainers."

Seppa Arroyo's account of the physical layouts of the outcall operations, and the working conditions at the agencies, suggests something akin to a telemarketing "boiler room."

> *The offices each consisted of seven to nine rooms, including phone rooms, managers' offices, record-keeping rooms, computer rooms, and supply rooms. In addition, the office at Sweethearts had a kitchen, a security room, and a training room, while the office at Playmates had a small employee restroom. The main room in each office was the phone room, where the phone girls sat and answered incoming calls and the dancers dropped off money after each appointment. Each phone room had four desks with a switchboard-style phone on each desk. The phones had approximately fifty separate telephone lines on them, and each line was*

advertised with the name of a different agency or supposedly independent entertainer. Each phone line was marked so that the office staff immediately knew which ad a customer was calling on every time the phone rang.

The phone rooms also had safes in them, which were bolted to the ground, with a slot for cash to be dropped in. Workers did not know the combinations to the safes, and we were encouraged to think of the safes as bottomless holes. Once the money was dropped in it ceased to exist. If a phone girl's tip was dropped into the safe, either by accident or because of a lack of change, it would not be refunded.

The offices were both completely wired with audiovisual surveillance, as are all major outcall agencies in the Las Vegas area. At both agencies, the focus of the cameras and microphones was the phone room since both types of assets that could be stolen from the company, information and cash, came directly into that room. Customers' names and locations were written on legal pads that were provided by the agencies. Staff members were never allowed to remove pads from the office. Pads were reviewed, page by page, by management during every shift. At Sweethearts, the pads were filed in a locked office. At Playmates, the pages were shredded after the managers reviewed them.

At Sweethearts, the procedure for allowing an employee, dancer, or any other person into the office involved listening for the outside doorbell, buzzing only known persons into the building and ensuring that they were not *accompanied by any other persons by viewing the outside security camera, waiting for the individual in questions to ring the inside doorbell, rechecking their identity on the indoor security camera, and buzzing them into the offices. At Playmates, dancers were only allowed into the office when they filled out their applications. Dancers dropped the agency fees they collected through a slot in the door.*

Seppa Arroyo said in her thesis that the number of successful calls handled by an individual agency in a given night varied greatly but, in her experience, it usually numbered between fifty and seventy-five calls per shift on a Friday or Saturday evening. Call volumes were generally lower on weekdays. Those numbers fit with Eddie Munoz reporting about a hundred calls a day to his service, on average.

Typically, an outcall transaction would work this way: a customer would call a service and, depending on which ad they were looking at, request a particular type of woman. Such as a "Coquettish College Girl" or one of those "Blond Asian MILFs" mentioned earlier in this book.

The service would look at its roster of working girls and pick one that most closely matched the request. The "entertainer" (escort) would be paged and she would call in to the service to verify she was available and start making her way to the customer.

Once she got to the client's home or hotel room, the first thing the escort would do was explain the financial arrangements. First, she had to collect the "agency fee" which, in the 1990s, ranged from $150 to $300, depending on the agency and whether the customer was paying cash or using a credit card. The agency fee was what the sex worker paid the outcall agency to handle the advertising and defray other costs, which might include the wages of the phone girls who booked the calls. Once that fee was paid, the escort would negotiate with the customers for the actual sex act. Here, depending on what the customer wanted, and for how long, the costs could range from $500 to $5,000. The money given to the "entertainer" over and above the agency fee was known in the industry as the entertainer's "tip."

The agency fee, meanwhile, helped insulate the owners of the outcall services from prosecution. Should an escort be caught in a Metro police vice sting (where undercover cops posed as johns in hotel rooms), the agency owner could simply say, "She's an independent contractor, not an employee. She pays me a flat fee for referrals, but I had no idea she was going to that hotel room to do anything other than perform an exotic dance." To further insulate themselves from culpability, escort service owners generally had the "entertainers" sign statements to the effect that they would not engage in prostitution.

Like the French police captain in the movie *Casablanca* who is "shocked to discover gambling going on here" as he collects his winnings, the outcall service owners also routinely expressed shock that their "entertainers" turned out to be hookers. The argument was laughable, but just plausible enough to prevent the major players in the escort industry from ever being convicted of felony pandering charges.

In order to keep their denials plausible, the outcall agency owners had to cut ties with any so-called entertainers caught up in a Metro vice sting. But this happened to relatively few women because the stings were costly to set up and once a hotel room was identified by the services as being the site of a sting, the agencies would call or fax each other with the information, so no other escorts were sent to the location in a given evening.

Sometimes, vice cops might make only a couple of misdemeanor prostitution arrests in an entire night before word of the room setup leaked out and no other escorts would come. The sting operations, which generally included the use of a hidden police video camera, made for entertaining episodes of police reality shows, but were time consuming and did little to cramp the style of the outcall agency owners.

Of all the escort service owners in Las Vegas in the 1990s, the most prominent was undoubtedly Richard Soranno. Originally from New Jersey, Soranno had at one time been, like many of the early outcall entrepreneurs, an exotic dancer himself. In the 1980s, he was a regular fixture at a club called "Bogeys" on the Las Vegas Strip, which featured male strip tease. Soranno billed himself as the "Italian Stallion."

"He had a real edge to him," remembers author Jack Sheehan, who interviewed Soranno for Sheehan's book *Skin City*. "He didn't get threatening, but he tried to be a little intimidating. He wanted me to know he was a powerful guy and he controlled a lot of women and he controlled a lot of money."

Years before sitting down with Soranno for his book, Sheehan first saw him at a party in Las Vegas in the early 1980s, during Soranno's performing days. "And, wow, was that pretty crazy," Sheehan said. "There was some full-on sex going on with twenty-five people watching. It was nuts, with a lot of $20 and $100 bills floating around."

But Soranno's talent as a performer was nothing in comparison to the genius he would later demonstrate as an outcall impresario. After he hung up his G-string, Soranno went into business as an outcall promoter and service owner. He employed legions of pamphleteers to spread his promotional materials on The Strip sidewalks and was one of the first outcall service owners to use the internet for advertising.

He fought high-profile legal battles with Metro and Clark County regulators while professing the legitimacy of his operations. He stood on the First Amendment and said that all he was doing was dispatching entertainers to hotel rooms to dance, which was a constitutionally protected form of freedom of expression (what happened between the dancer and the hotel guest after freedom was expressed was their business).

Soranno's business acumen and his persistence paid off. He became more than a millionaire. And when the roll of successful outcall agency owners was called, Soranno found himself at the top of the list.

But his Horatio Alger-like success would also land him on top of another list, according to investigators, a list compiled by associates of New York's Gambino and Bonanno La Cosa Nostra families: the roster of Las Vegas outcall promoters who might have to be taken out—when the Mafia muscled in.

Chapter Five

On Uncle Sam's Escort Service

In the annals of crime fighting, police use of "sting" techniques dates back as far as the early 1700s and the exploits of London's Jonathan Wild, a notorious fence who bought stolen goods—but also worked with police to bring to justice some of the thieves he did business with.

One of the more common types of sting involves a storefront operation where police open a small business and set themselves up as either a pawnshop or second-hand store. Then, the undercover officers put the word out that they're buying stolen goods and the crooks end up coming to them. The undercover work sometimes goes on for the better part of a year and often results in hundreds of arrests, with perhaps millions of dollars in stolen property being returned to its rightful owners.

Other types of stings involve the hotel room setups described earlier in this book where cops pose as johns to catch hookers. The use of "bait cars" is another form of sting, wherein police leave vehicles—wired for video and audio—on the street as a temptation for car thieves. When the thief takes the bait, the cops can disable the vehicle by remote control and lock the thief in the car until they can be cuffed and arrested.

But of all the various types of undercover operations in the history of law enforcement, nobody could ever remember a federal agent being inserted as a "manager" into an actual, functioning escort service. That is, until escort service owner Tony Nastasi went to the Las Vegas FBI in November of 1997.

"No, I don't believe that's ever been done before," recalls retired FBI Special Agent Charles Maurer, who supervised the escort service operation.

"Oh, it was unique," said Maurer's former co-case Agent Jerry Hanford. "It was one of the strangest things I've done in the Bureau. I'd done a lot of undercovers, but that was bizarre."

FBI Special Agent Dan DeSimone was brought in from an FBI office on the east coast to act as Nastasi's manager in the escort service. And the key word here is act. Police sting operations over the years had shown most, if not the vast majority, of escort agencies were nothing but fronts for prostitution, so having an undercover agent in an escort service could be tricky. The FBI did not want, when the case was finally over, to be seen as having done anything that promoted prostitution.

"That was part of the stipulation we had to put in the proposal to have headquarters approve it. The appearance of us being involved in prostitution wouldn't be good, so we avoided all the business aspects of it," Maurer said.

The thirty-something Agent DeSimone had been with the Bureau about a decade and had done undercover work before. But he had never been in an undercover role that was so deep or so potentially long-lasting. He would ultimately pose as an escort service manager for the better part of a year. And there was a vital reason the FBI wanted the undercover agent (UCA) to be from out of town.

"I came from the east coast and it was important to ensure that I didn't have any family or relatives in the area that I could accidentally cross paths with or bump into that could accidentally cause a disruption of the operation by referring to me as someone else," DeSimone said, in an interview for this book.

"I did not have any family or friends there (Las Vegas) so that was part of the overall way of ensuring that we would have, hopefully, no chance encounters with anyone who would know me by my real identity."

DeSimone said he did not simply move to Las Vegas and immediately go to work posing as an escort service employee. Before the curtain went up on his undercover operation, he underwent a considerable amount of training and briefings about the people he was likely to encounter.

According to retired Agent Charles Maurer, DeSimone was a manager in name only at Nastasi's Casablanca West escort service, and rarely even visited the office. DeSimone's job was to get introduced to all the players in the escort industry and collect intelligence about the workings of the call girl racket. DeSimone's nom-de-outcall was C. Daniel Borelli, and there were business cards printed up with his fake, undercover name. He went by "Dan" or "Danny" to the suspected wiseguys he met.

"Dan had to make it appear he was doing something when he really wasn't doing anything," Maurer said. "He might have presented himself as a manager, and Tony backed him up, but as far as people working there, I don't know if they ever saw him."

As for whether Nastasi continued sending out escorts while working as an informant, Maurer isn't sure.

"You know, I don't know. There wasn't much going on at all. I guess he might have, but I don't think he did though, because there was no business."

Retired agent Hanford believes that even with Nastasi's business being virtually non-existent, the FBI may have been pushing the envelope with regard to actually being in the escort trade since Nastasi still had women working for him throughout the operation.

"Tony Nastasi was working for us and, indirectly, they (his employees) were working for us. So, we kinda stretched the limits," Hanford observes.

The investigation had started out as a public corruption case, after Nastasi came to the FBI with claims he'd been approached by Las Vegas Metro vice detectives for protection money during Nastasi's arrest on pandering charges. But information quickly developed that added an organized crime element to the probe, while at the same time fueling concerns about possible corruption in both the police department and the Clark County District Attorney's office.

Following his release from jail, but before his trial on the pandering charge, Nastasi got a phone call, completely out of the blue, from a surprising source.

Here's how Agent Maurer described what happened in a 1998 search warrant application, in which undercover agent Dan DeSimone is designated (UCA) and Nastasi is named as Cooperating Witness number one (CW-1):

> *Shortly after his release, CW-1 (Nastasi) was contacted by an individual named Christiano DeCarlo, who was previously unknown to the CW-1. DeCarlo claimed that he is connected to Vincent Faraci and John Conti, both of whom are known to the FBI as members of the LCN, and that DeCarlo could help CW-1 with the pending charges.*
>
> *Faraci is the son of John Faraci, also known as Johnny Green, who is an acting capo in the Bonanno LCN family. Faraci is known to have recently borrowed $100,000 from John Gotti, Jr., and it also appears from investigations conducted by the FBI that the Gambino LCN family is behind the attempt to gain control of the Las Vegas outcall industry. Investigation determined that DeCarlo is also an outcall*

service operator in Las Vegas. CW-1 agreed to assist the FBI in this investigation and to permit the FBI to place an undercover FBI agent (UCA) to pose as an employee of his Las Vegas business.

In June of 1998, a meeting was arranged between DeCarlo, CW-1, and the UCA.

During this conversation, DeCarlo detailed his involvement in the outcall business and agreed to assist the CW in fixing his pending case. DeCarlo told CW-1 to return to New York and await contact from someone there. Shortly after returning to New York, CW-1 was contacted by an individual who identified himself as "Mario." Mario has been identified as Mario Pugliesi, a Gambino LCN family associate. Pugliesi arranged a meeting with CW-1 during which he agreed to assist the CW-1 with his case if CW-1 "checked out." In the meantime, the UCA contacted Vincent Faraci in Las Vegas.

Faraci told the UCA that he would do business with the UCA later if everything checked out and a formal introduction was made by the right people.

In early August of 1998, CW-1 was again contacted by Pugliesi in New York. Pugliesi told CW-1 that he had looked into the CW-1's background and he was now prepared to deal with him. Another meeting between CW-1 and Pugliesi was set for August 17, 1998.

During this meeting, Pugliesi stated that he could assist CW-1 in fixing his case but the cost to CW-1 would be $25,000. After some negotiation by CW-1, Pugliesi agreed to accept $10,000, which Pugliesi claimed would cover only the "costs" of taking care of CW-1's case. Pugliesi also stated that he could arrange to increase the amount of business at CW-1's Las Vegas outcall service in return for a share of the profits. CW-1 complained to Pugliesi about some of his competitors in Las Vegas, namely Frank Bartello and Richard Soranno. Pugliesi replied that he was aware of both of those individuals and that a couple aspirins will be sent to Las Vegas to deal with those 'headaches.'

The meetings between Pugliesi and CW-1 were surveilled by agents of the New York Office of the FBI. Pugliesi told CW-1 that he used to be "with Roy DeMeo," who was a Gambino LCN family capo with a reputation for violence. DeMeo is now deceased. Pugliesi added that the people with whom he is now connected are 'crazier than DeMeo.'

After consideration of the severity of the criminal activity and the potential for violence by the subjects, FBI authority was obtained to make the $10,000 payment. Consequently, on August 20, 1998, the UCA met with DeCarlo and paid the $10,000. A lengthy consensually recorded conversation took place during this meeting in which DeCarlo discussed the plans that he and Pugliesi had made in regard to the future of the outcall business in Las Vegas. DeCarlo stated that he had been working on behalf of Pugliesi for about a year and a half and that he had checked out all the major players in the outcall business, particularly to *determine if they had any LCN affiliations with other cities. DeCarlo told the UCA that he had hesitated to help CW-1 because he was afraid of risking any "heat" at this very crucial time, but that he had agreed because Pugliesi said that there could be long term advantages. DeCarlo stated that in the near future individuals would be sent to deal with Bartello, Soranno, and another unnamed outcall service operator. They would each be given a choice between giving over control of their businesses to DeCarlo or being killed. DeCarlo stated that he persuaded Pugliesi not to kill all three at one time because, although such a crime might go unnoticed in New York City, the death of three outcall service operators in Las Vegas in a short period of time would call attention to them. DeCarlo told the UCA that Las Vegas is not used to this type of activity, referring to the proposed murders.*

Undercover agent Dan DeSimone, posing as outcall manager Danny Borelli, remembers the conversation with DeCarlo about the prospect of whacking the top players in the Las Vegas outcall industry in order to put the others in line.

"My first real, substantive meeting with DeCarlo took place at Caesars' Palace at Spago over lunch," DeSimone said. "And, you know, that's the time where he looked at me and said, 'Hey, you know, this isn't New York out here, I keep telling the people back east. We can't just take three of these outcall owners, take 'em all out in the desert and kill 'em. That's gonna make the news.' His kinda thought process was, well, we'll take one of them out there and if they don't pay us what we think they owe us, we'll kill him and the other two will kinda get the message and pay us what we think they owe us."

No matter what you thought of the escort trade, there were real people running these businesses who appeared to be at risk of death or serious bodily harm, and the FBI had to take the perceived threats seriously.

Fortunately, the FBI now had an informant who was running an escort service with an undercover federal agent as his ersatz manager.

Tony Nastasi's business bona fides were apparently impressive enough to convince Mario Pugliese (also known by his alias of Mario Stefano) to enlist Nastasi in the suspected scheme to take over outcall services in Las Vegas. No doubt the $10,000 payment (from undercover FBI coffers) to help "fix" Nastasi's pandering case was also persuasive. People will talk, but when money talks, people listen.

Although the offer to fix Nastasi's case might have been mere puffery on the part of Pugliese, a con game to squeeze ten grand out of Nastasi, the offer itself, the fact that Nastasi was approached about his case by a man with Mob connections he'd never met before, and the remarks Nastasi said Metro vice cops made about paying them for protection, all pointed to the possibility that someone in law enforcement had been compromised.

"The contact from DeCarlo was completely unsolicited by the cooperating witness," said former agent Maurer. "So, the cooperating witness was sure that it had something to do with the remark made by the police officer (allegedly, about paying protection money)."

Investigators say DeCarlo also assured Nastasi that in addition to having his pandering case go away, as an added bonus, Nastasi would also get tipped off about upcoming Metro vice stings in hotel rooms thanks to DeCarlo's supposed connections in law enforcement.

"He (DeCarlo) said he could get his (Nastasi's) case fixed and, in the future, he could tell the cooperating witness in advance whenever Metro set up a sting," retired agent

Maurer said. "He claimed to have contacts in the Metro police department that would contact him and warn him, so his 'entertainers' could avoid the sting."

It wasn't conclusive evidence of corruption, but it was enough to prompt the federal agents to dig deeper and seek warrants for wiretaps that might catch the main players implicating themselves over the telephone.

The court-authorized wiretaps, along with recordings made consensually by Nastasi and DeSimone in person, with body-worn audio recorders, would eventually provide agents with a vast collection of evidence against the alleged Mob associates. The recordings would paint a picture of greed, callousness, and back-stabbing among the conspirators as the pressure mounted to succeed in the escort industry takeover plot.

That associates of a New York crime family would target Las Vegas escort services may seem less surprising than the fact it took them this long to make the move.

"Well, the Gambino family trying to come into outcall services shows a couple of things. One, it's incredibly profitable," said UNLV's Michael Green. "Why get into it if you're not going to make money at it? Two, it's important to Las Vegas. If they didn't think they'd make money at it in Las Vegas, why bother coming in from New York?"

Tony Nastasi, who was also from New York, dutifully played the role of Mob-connected outcall agency owner in order to get the conspirators to reveal more about their plans for a suspected Vegas takeover. In addition to paying the $10,000 to fix his court case, Nastasi made regular phone calls to Pugliesi back in The Big Apple. Nastasi also visited Pugliese in person during trips back to New York, sometimes discussing the cut-throat nature of the outcall business in Las Vegas.

In one conversation, recorded without Pugliese's knowledge, Nastasi complains that DeCarlo—who had supposedly claimed inside connections with Metro police—

has not been providing him with advance information about Metro vice operations.

"He (DeCarlo) said he had the 'in' on that, that his office would call me when the bulls are around," Nastasi said on the recording. "There was a pinch last night at Bally's and in The Oasis. Now, according to him, what he said was, he would give us a call because he knows when all these things are about to happen. He gets the word. Well, we never got word. We almost sent somebody to Bally's last night and we woulda got pinched."

Pugliese, who seemed a sort of a father figure to DeCarlo (to whom he refers as "the kid" because DeCarlo was only 27 at the time), suggests Nastasi cut the kid some slack. According to Pugliese, DeCarlo had lost considerable business to the big players in Las Vegas, which included Richard Soranno, Frank Bartello, and possibly two other outcall owners, Harry Jacobs and Anthony Cecola.

"He got banged up pretty good with these guys, they hurt him pretty good," Pugliese said in the secretly made recording. "Evidently, they're fucking up his phones, where now they don't steal the calls—which they're doing with you—but they're not stealing his, but…"

Nastasi interrupts: "They're re-routing them. I know they're doing something because it's impossible—with the advertising we got—that we should not be a lot bigger that what we are, you know what I'm saying?"

Here, the phone call diversion scheme is mentioned, though no one is named as the culprit behind the scheme. It seems clear, however, that Mob associates suspect whoever was behind the alleged call diversion was working for one or more of the top outcall entertainment promoters.

"There was a strong belief in the mind of DeCarlo, conveyed to others back east, that somehow these other adult entertainment operators had messed with the phones and were diverting business to these other adult entertainment agencies," said former undercover agent Dan DeSimone.

"And it was causing DeCarlo to lose a lot of money and he would note that this was negatively impacting the folks back east—which would give one the premise that, you know, is he paying people back east? Is he sending (them) a percentage of his business?"

Whether the interest from Pugliese, and perhaps others back east, was paternal or financial was a question the FBI wanted answered.

DeCarlo made no secret of the fact that he felt his business had been disrupted by the top Las Vegas outcall service owners and that disruption was, in his mind, due to the interception of phone calls meant for his own escort service.

"When that dried up, he engaged Mario Stefano (Pugliese) for help, and the plot was undertaken," said DeSimone.

In the previously mentioned phone call, intercepted by FBI agents, Pugliese (aka Stefano) promised Nastasi he'd do something to teach the major players in the Vegas escort industry a lesson.

Again, from the secretly made recording, we hear from Pugliese:

> *Well, you know what it is. We know they're doing the same shit that they did to him (DeCarlo) to you. So, we're going down, straighten things out for you and him. I got three guys goin' down there and I wanna see what I can do to straighten it out with these assholes, these punks that they are, you know what I mean? They'll get a lesson.*

The first of the three men dispatched by Pugliese was Kenneth Byrnes. Byrnes, a bearish and colorful man, had been the subject of a *New York* magazine article less than two years prior to the events unfolding in Las Vegas. In that article, Byrnes admitted being the target of a 1996 Internal Revenue Service undercover operation, based out of Dallas,

Texas, with the not-so-imaginative title of "Operation Out-call."

Essentially, Byrnes and his associates were accused of creating a system that would allow johns to pay hookers with credit cards without the credit card bills indicating prostitution was involved.

Byrnes' company would accept the credit card payments, take a small percentage out for providing the service, then pay the prostitutes or pimps in cash.

Byrnes suggested he and his partners were helping to clean up the escort industry. If, by "clean up," he meant "launder," then the feds agreed with him. Federal prosecutors labeled what he did money laundering.

From the *New York* story:

> The prospect of several years in a federal penitentiary seems to have sharpened Kenneth Byrnes' self-awareness.
>
> 'I've been involved in a lot of stupid things in my life, but this takes the cake,' he acknowledges. 'I'm one of those pie-in-the-sky guys. I get involved in these screwball schemes that blow up in my face.'
>
> Byrnes is a big guy, six three and maybe 300 pounds, and when he says "screwball schemes" you think Ralph Kramden's glow-in-the-dark wallpaper. But according to government affidavits, the thirty-five-year-old New Jersey man is a central figure in what is becoming the most sweeping prostitution case in US law-enforcement history. Snared in Operation Outcall, a huge and ongoing Internal Revenue Service sting, Byrnes is alleged to be the brains—to the extent that there were any brains—behind Entertainment Management Services, Inc., a Paramus-based

company that processed and laundered more than $16 million in prostitution credit-card charges.

Byrnes and his two partners (one an attorney under suspension from the New Jersey Supreme Court and the other a retired executive with heart trouble) spent more than a year working and sharing business secrets with men who turned out to be undercover IRS agents.

The trio was recorded in more than 500 telephone calls and eight face-to-face meetings with agents, including one in which a partner actually bragged, "I'm running a national-prostitution-money-laundering ring, [and] all our clients are pimps and madams.'

"He certainly was self-aware at how incompetent his team had been," said Daniel Green, author of the "New York" story about Byrnes, in an interview for this book.

"I got a sense that he was one of those guys who was not stupid. I just think the plan was not all that clever."

Green said he didn't stay in touch with Byrnes after the 1996 article, and he was unaware Byrnes had gone on to become embroiled later in yet another undercover federal investigation involving escort services, in Las Vegas.

."I kinda wish I had because I liked the guy. You know, we had a good time and he was a very friendly, likeable, and—it's strange to say—but almost innocent guy."

Green said when he interviewed Byrnes in a New Jersey diner in 1996 for the IRS story, Byrnes was quite willing to talk openly about his own role in the money laundering caper.

"He thought he hadn't done anything wrong and I think he believed anyone who heard his story wouldn't believe he had done anything wrong," Green said.

Yet, despite his public, self-recrimination in the article over involvement in a scheme involving prostitution and escort services, Byrnes would find himself in Las Vegas less than two years later, once again in the thick of the escort industry, and once again—without knowing it—at the heart of a federal, criminal investigation. Being involved in two, separate criminal cases centering on prostitution seems to fly in the face of the impression Byrnes gave of being merely an earnest, but possibly naive, businessman caught up in something he did not understand to be a crime.

In the Las Vegas case, as in New Jersey, Byrnes would again be sharing confidences with an undercover federal agent as well as a civilian federal informant. Byrnes' so-called pie-in-the-sky schemes were poised to become a very real pie in the face, with consequences that would likely include a stretch in a federal penitentiary.

Daniel DeSimone, the FBI agent working undercover as a supposed escort service manager, remembers meeting Byrnes for the first time. DeSimone said Byrnes "arrived as described." He was a big man, six foot four-ish, DeSimone recalls.

"And definitely the kind of guy who would be an offensive lineman in the National Football League," said DeSimone. "So, his stature was intimidating in nature, his voice commanded a level of authority, and his presence was one that would definitely be intimidating to an average-sized person."

DeSimone made it known that although Byrnes seemed genuinely gregarious, the undercover agent also sensed an undertone of danger surrounding him.

"You know, we all have tools in the jobs that we work in," DeSimone said. "His main tool was aluminum baseball bats. And it was strongly inferred, and kinda mentioned under the breath, that Ken is not afraid to—and has—used those bats to inflict harm on folks.

"So, while it may have looked like he was with the traveling softball team and coming to Vegas for a tournament, this kind of tournament was probably the potential to cause bodily harm to some folks."

Though he had not been indicted in the IRS sting by the time he flew to Las Vegas at Pugliese's behest, Byrnes still had the money laundering investigation hanging over his head. That investigation would surface in the Las Vegas outcall probe when some of Byrnes' associates were caught on a hidden microphone discussing whether Byrnes might be vulnerable to being "rolled" by the feds.

But for now, Byrnes would be Pugliese's advance man in Las Vegas. Byrnes' previous exposure to the escort industry would almost certainly help him collect intelligence about the major operators in Vegas and make it easier for him to determine who might be diverting phone calls away from Mob-backed outcall services.

Although nobody knew who the mastermind behind the alleged call diversion scheme actually was at this point, a plausible perpetrator soon emerged within the organized crime community. It was a man whose curious history of working both sides of the law—and his keen sense of how computers and telephones worked—made him an obvious suspect.

But Charles Coveney, the man the alleged Mob associates would eventually finger as the call diversion mastermind, was not obvious in his whereabouts. This middle-aged computer nerd, who had conducted electronic "black bag" capers for both cops and capos, had taken elaborate precautions to stay one step ahead of both the Mob and the FBI. Finding Coveney would prove no easy job for either gangsters or G-men.

Chapter Six

Man of Mystery

Charles Coveney was an open book on a hidden shelf. Some of his exploits as an electronic surveillance expert made headlines, and his own name appeared in the stories beneath the headlines. Under an assumed name, it's said he produced an Emmy-winning TV show about the covert interception of communications. He did work for state, local, and federal police agencies. But he also did off-the-books black bag operations for casino owners and shadowy figures with Mob connections. His expertise was well known in both the law-enforcement and organized crime communities. Exactly what he did with his specialized skills—and for whom—was not always known. And, like TV's fictional *A-Team*, you might be able to hire him—if you could find him.

Shortly before his death in 2012, I conducted what is likely the only interview Charles Coveney ever gave about the alleged attempt by a Mafia family to take control of the call girl racket in Las Vegas in 1998.

Coveney had called me and asked if I wanted to talk about the events of nearly fifteen years prior. Though I had left journalism and was working as a staff investigator for the Federal Public Defender of Nevada, I couldn't refuse an opportunity to talk to the man I'd tried for years to track down when I was covering the story. I took a day off and went to see him at the address he provided.

By this time, Coveney was severely diabetic and had gone blind due to complications from heart surgery. He was living in a casita behind a modest, mid-century modern house in the John S. Park neighborhood of Las Vegas, one of the oldest neighborhoods in Vegas and not far from downtown. He allowed me to tape-record our interview but didn't want a camera used because he felt vulnerable and didn't want anyone to know what he looked like at the time.

Coveney told me he was generally working in one of two places in 1998: Binion's Horseshoe Casino or at *El Mundo*, the city's largest Spanish-language newspaper. *El Mundo* was published by the late Eddie Escobedo, a pioneer in businesses catering to Latinos in Las Vegas, and Coveney spent a lot of time at the newspaper.

"He told me he was a beta tester for Apple," remembers Mike Bindrup, who met Coveney at *El Mundo*. Bindrup, a native Las Vegan and business consultant who spoke fluent Spanish, was involved with creating Spanish-language newspaper ads for various Las Vegas companies. Bindrup soon discovered he shared a mutual, high-tech interest with Coveney: computers and computer programming.

"He used to test Apple products," Bindrup said. "And so, he would have the latest, greatest software."

Coveney had a sharp mind for computers, Bindrup recalls, but was hardly a sharp dresser. From a personal appearance standpoint, Bindrup said, Coveney was mostly a mess.

"He had scraggly long hair and a scraggly beard. He was always dressed in the same kind of outfit: he wore cargo shorts, with extra pockets, and he always had on a t-shirt with a 'tech' logo, like an Apple shirt. But it was always crisply ironed."

Bindrup would drive Coveney around town since Coveney didn't own a car. In fact, one of the few available pictures of Coveney during this time is his Metro Police mug shot made during an arrest for driving without a valid license. That booking photo is included in this book.

One day, while chauffeuring Coveney around town, Bindrup couldn't resist asking Coveney why he was so personally unkempt, but his t-shirts were always pressed. Coveney said it was a perk of living (off the books) at Binion's Horseshoe Hotel.

"He lived there. He ate there," Bindrup said. "He had laundry service. And they would press his clothes."

Coveney told Bindrup he'd been sent to Las Vegas by a major New York news organization to collect information for a hit piece on Benny Binion, patriarch of the Binion gambling empire and a man with his own links to organized crime. But instead of producing material for a hit piece, Binion and Coveney hit it off, with Coveney becoming a security consultant for Binion and helping to get Binion's *World Series of Poker* on national TV.

"And when Benny died, he left it in his will or something that he (Coveney) could stay there as long as he wanted to," Bindrup said. At least that's the story Coveney told Bindrup.

"I thought he was retired. I thought he was retired from RKO Radio," said David Raymond, former partner in Renie and Raymond Computers, which had its office downtown in the Manpower building on Las Vegas Boulevard. Raymond met Coveney through the computer business as a salesman. He said he never saw any indication that Coveney had connections to the escort industry or the Mafia, though Coveney was fond of using an Italian American slang word that ended up becoming his own moniker.

"We called him 'Charlie the Chooch'," Raymond remembers. "That name was the name he used on everybody else—so we ended up putting that name back on him."

"Chooch" is a term that means "jackass."

Like Mike Bindrup, David Raymond quickly discovered that Coveney, or "Charlie the Chooch" always had the latest computer programs.

"He would get his hands on a lot of software. It wasn't pirated software; it was actual software with proper licenses. I don't know how he did it."

Raymond said there's no question Coveney had close connections to Binion's Horseshoe.

"He knew people at Binion's, and he would invite us for dinner there quite often. He was always getting comps."

As for whether "Charlie the Chooch" actually lived at Binion's, Raymond is doubtful, although he said Coveney never told anyone where he actually lived.

"Each time we tried to take him home he always had us drop him off two blocks away from his house. Downtown."

Although Binion's Horseshoe is located in downtown Las Vegas, Raymond said the spots where he and others dropped Coveney off were not real close to Binion's. Still, it was possible to walk there from those locations, so he can't rule out the possibility that the Horseshoe was, in fact, Coveney's home.

Chip Falcon is the pseudonym for another IT and computer consultant who knew Coveney but did not want his real name used in this book. Falcon met Coveney through Renie and Raymond computers, and Falcon said he, too, was kept in the dark about where Coveney lived. So, he also can't dismiss the suggestion that Coveney's home might have been Binion's Horseshoe Hotel and Casino.

"I used to drop him off downtown and he never alluded to where he was going. He just said, 'Drop me off at the corner.' I'm sure it's possible (Binion's Horseshoe was his home)."

Coveney's story about how he came to be essentially a semi-secret, recurring guest at Binion's Horseshoe may be apocryphal; a load of something that begins with the word "horse" but doesn't end with the word "shoe." Nevertheless, there are stories of special friends of Benny Binion living surreptitiously in a wing or floor of the Horseshoe Hotel. Among them, supposedly, was former Dallas wiseguy

R.D. Matthews. Matthews was an associate of Jack Ruby, the man who killed suspected JFK assassin Lee Harvey Oswald shortly after the president's murder in Dallas in 1963. Matthews's name made headlines a few years later, when his business card was found in the pocket of hitman Charles Harrelson, father of actor Woody Harrelson. The elder Harrelson was arrested for and later convicted of, the murder of a federal judge in Texas in 1969.

Whether he lived there or not, Coveney had close connections to Binion's Horseshoe. Mike Bindrup said he would often drop Coveney off at the Horseshoe, where the computer programmer would play poker for hours on end.

"When I wasn't at Binion's, and doing stuff at Binion's, and hanging around Binion's," Coveney told me in our 2012 interview, "I was dealing with Escobedo, teaching his people how to operate computers."

Coveney told me he got word from Escobedo that FBI agents wanted to talk to him after agents dropped by *El Mundo* looking for the computer expert. This was late in the FBI's investigation; perhaps a day or two before it came to an end.

"Eddie reached out to me and he said, 'Two FBI agents were here looking for you,'" Coveney told me. "'They wanna know where the hell you're living. They have to talk to you right away.' I said ok."

Coveney called the FBI and arranged to meet Special Agents Charles Maurer and Jerry Hanford at the Blueberry Hill Pancake House a few blocks east of the FBI building on East Charleston Boulevard. Coveney chose the restaurant because he knew agents often had breakfast there.

From my recorded interview with Coveney:

> Coveney: *I said, I'll be there at nine o'clock. So, I got there at seven. 'Cause I know how these guys work (laughs). Anyway, I see 'em setting up.*

Glen Meek: *So, they're setting up like a counter surveillance...?*

Coveney: *Yeah, they were setting up surveillance; they wanted to identify where I was at. They actually wanted to know where I was living. 'Cause they had no idea where I was, and I actually believe that to be true— that they had no idea where I was living. So, as a result of that I'm there and these two guys show up and one comes over and sits down with me and I said, how you doing and so forth and so on.*

Coveney: *He said, 'You know we have a problem; we got some people looking for you.' I said, 'Ok, for what?' They said, 'Well, they seem to think you have the ability to tap phones.' I said, 'Well, probably true. I do have that ability.' Anyway, I said, 'I have done that in the past. Of course, your office would be well aware of that if you wanted to call Washington and check me out. Please be my guest.'*

Coveney told me the federal agents informed him that he might be in danger because they believed organized crime figures had people looking for him. The Mob-connected guys believed Coveney was the brains behind a phone call diversion scam, agents said. Coveney's name had surfaced late in the case, although the supposed wiseguys had been complaining about call diversion for months prior to Coveney being named as the likely suspect in the scheme.

Coveney told the agents, "I said, how would I know that? I'm not involved in that, I wouldn't know about that."

Coveney was adamant with the FBI, and later, me, that he had nothing to do with intercepting phone calls meant for one escort service and diverting them to another. But he freely admitted—and practically bragged—that he had the knowledge and resources to do it.

"He gave us kind of a two-sided answer," remembers retired agent Hanford. "No, he wasn't doing it. But could it be done? Yeah, probably could be done."

Hanford's memory of the meeting with Coveney hews closely to the version Coveney gave me.

Hanford said he and agent Maurer went to the meeting to give Coveney a warning that he might be in danger, and to find out what he might know about the alleged call diversion.

"We wanted to make it clear to him that there were people threatening him, and we were letting him know."

Though the FBI agents also wanted to enlist Coveney's help in their investigation, Coveney wanted no part of it.

"I said, well, first of all, I don't need your protection, number one. Number two, I don't need your help. And, I'm not interested in getting involved in your case. Good luck with it. I hope you get the guys."

Coveney went on to tell me in our 2012 interview, "I wasn't trying to be cute with them, but I'm not in a situation where I wanna get involved in this at all. I have no idea how my name was even mentioned, that I had the ability to do this."

Coveney told me he believed someone in the FBI had floated his name to the underworld as being the call diversion mastermind. Interestingly, a rogue FBI agent did resign from the Las Vegas office in late 1997, and that former agent was indicted in 2000, for supplying inside FBI information to Mob associates or their criminal defense attorneys. However, it's never been alleged that any of the secrets the disgraced former agent sold to mobsters were connected to the Las Vegas outcall case.

Despite Coveney's denials to me and the FBI, there is one knowledgeable person who remains convinced Coveney was, in fact, involved in a call diversion scheme. That person is in a position to know. His name is Bill Coveney.

He's Charles Coveney's older brother, and a retired federal agent with the U.S. Customs Service.

"I do know that he was doing something like that," Bill Coveney told me in an interview for this book. "And when I moved here (Las Vegas), I was already retired from Customs. That's why he was a little more open with me."

"He did say he was involved with something like that. But he never said with whom or for whom. He never told me that," Bill Coveney said.

"It was call diversion. He said he had a guy in Sprint, at the time, he was paying off, or paying money to."

As for Charles Coveney's name surfacing as the man behind the call diversion, Bill Coveney suspects it was wiseguys talking to one another, not a federal agent leaking information.

Bill said his brother Charles had his own Mob connections going back to the early 1960s, when the men were growing up together in New Jersey.

"Union County, New Jersey, when he was young, seventeen or eighteen-years old, he became a collector for the local Mob, and went around to the bars and collected protection money from the bar keepers in Union County. That's how he got involved."

The elder Coveney said his sibling Charles eventually graduated from collecting extortion payments in bars where he was too young to legally order a drink and began to perform more sophisticated work for various crime families, probably related to surveillance or the surreptitious recording of communications.

Charles' flirtation with the underworld manifested itself in some curious and sometime amusing ways, according to his brother. Charles liked to flash cash, Bill said, and bring people home to family gatherings who did not always fit in the well-to-do circles of upscale Summit, New Jersey, where their father was a vice president for Western Electric Corporation.

"Back in the early '60s, he brought home a guy that had just got out of prison, an Italian guy out of Brooklyn," Bill Coveney remembers. "And this guy came out of federal prison in San Diego for a twenty-ton load of marijuana that he brought up from Mexico."

Female friends Charles brought to his parent's house in Summit also ruffled some feathers.

"My mother almost died," Bill said. "He brought a Las Vegas showgirl in a see-through dress on a Sunday afternoon and my mother was choking. My father didn't know what to do."

Despite his fascination with the trappings of wiseguys and gangsters, at some point Charles drew a line between them and himself.

"He never made it into the Mafia," Bill Coveney said. "I don't think he wanted that. But he was being paid by the Mafia, doing things for them. The Mafia in New Jersey and New York City—the five families. He was very involved with the five families."

The work Charles did for the Mob was apparently similar to what he did for law-enforcement agencies although, presumably, the law-enforcement agencies went to the trouble to get court orders before tapping a telephone.

It was really no surprise that Charles Coveney became an expert at the covert interception and monitoring of wire communications. Charles was, in a fashion, born to the work. Western Electric, where Charles' father was a high-ranking executive, was the prime supplier of telecommunications equipment for the old Bell System, which had a monopoly on the nation's telephone network up until the 1980s.

This was a time when the Bell System was switching over to touch-tone dialing, which is essentially a computerized form of phone call switching. Charles' father's employer was involved in the computer upgrading of the telephone network in the 1960s and young Charles, no doubt, took a keen interest.

His use of his developing electronics skills on behalf of organized crime figures reveals a dark side of Charles Coveney, but he played both sides of the law, and helped numerous police agencies crack cases and send crooks to jail. Some of that work was chronicled in this obituary which ran in the *Las Vegas Review Journal* newspaper in May of 2012:

> *Charles 'Charlie' Coveney, passed away May 24, 2012, at his home in Las Vegas, after a prolonged illness. He was born on April 3, 1941, in Natick, Massachusetts, and was the second of seven children. He attended Summit High School in Summit, New Jersey. He was preceded in death by his parents, William and Marie Coveney; and his younger brother, Robert.*
>
> *In 1963, Charlie was a licensed private detective in New Jersey & was noted to be a natural at covert surveillance. He was often hired by spouses to conduct raids in order to prove adultery.*
>
> *Charlie subsequently was a state of New Jersey constable and developed many "sources" on the street. He was able to provide considerable information, while operating undercover, to local law enforcement agencies in Essex, Union, Somerset, and Middlesex Counties, as well as several of those counties' prosecutor's offices and detective bureaus. He also worked with the New Jersey State Police and other area law enforcement agencies, including the US Attorney's Office, the ATF, and the FBI. His work resulted in numerous arrests, successful prosecutions, and the recovery of stolen property, guns, narcotics, and money.*

In addition, he was a technical consultant to a number of law enforcement agencies, in the areas of Electronic Surveillance and countermeasures.

In the '80's and '90's, Charlie acted as a contract agent for a number of federal agencies (both domestically and abroad) in undercover capacities and assumed identities which are covered under non-disclosure due to national security endangerment. During that period, due to an undisclosed number of threats on Charlie's life, he went into hiding and lived under false identifications, Carlos McCarthy being the last known.

Charlie surfaced in Las Vegas, and began working for "El Mundo," the largest Spanish speaking news organization in Las Vegas. He gained the trust of a number of top casino owners in Las Vegas and became a security consultant to several of them. He assisted with internal and external security and with closed circuit video surveillance equipment.

Charlie produced the F. Lee Bailey Crime Show "The War Within," which won an Emmy. He was also instrumental in helping to establish relationships between ESPN and various casino operators. This led to the production and televising of the now famous ESPN World Series of Poker.

In 1999, he had heart surgery. Complications from the surgery eventually caused him to go blind. He subsequently obtained a service dog from Guiding Eyes for the Blind and "Lance" became Charlie's best friend.

"Charlie will be interned with his parents at St. Theresa Cemetery, Summit, New Jersey."

The obituary, apparently written with information provided by Coveney's family, does not mention a significant drug smuggling case in 1979 where Charles served as an undercover informant for the FBI. Coveney helped the feds put away members, or associates, of the "Black Tuna" smuggling ring out of Miami, Florida, which, at the time, was considered by authorities to be among the biggest pot importation organizations in America. The case involved not only drug charges, but also a plot to bribe a juror and possibly kill the federal judge in the case. Coveney's testimony was key in convicting multiple defendants.

According to a December 1979 *Associated Press* article, the wife of a principal in the smuggling ring was accused, along with two New Jersey men, of cooking up a scheme to bribe a female juror.

"Those three asked Coveney for help," the article said. "Coveney became the FBI informant."

"According to a search warrant affidavit, Coveney and the others met in New York and New Jersey during October and November. Coveney wore a hidden eavesdropping device," the article reports.

In addition to the Black Tuna case, the *Review Journal* obit also does not mention Charles Coveney having any connection with the Las Vegas FBI outcall investigation, even though his name surfaced in the indictments as the target of the alleged Mob associates seeking the source of the phone call diversion.

And, while disclaiming any involvement to me (and the FBI), Coveney did tell me during our interview he had no doubt that telephone calls to some escort services had been diverted. Coveney said the diversion, however, did not take place within the phone company.

"Yeah, there was no question there was call diversion, and it was very simple to be done," Coveney told me. "It was done internally in each hotel."

Coveney said he heard from his sources that a few technicians working for the companies that serviced the switchboards in several strip hotels were dating strippers who worked for the escort services. These technicians, Coveney said, had supposedly installed small electronic devices in the hotel switchboards during routine maintenance. These devices had been programmed to recognize an escort service telephone number when it was dialed from a room and route that call to the escort services which the technicians' girlfriends worked for. The device, Coveney suspected, could be programmed to turn itself on and off at odd hours. It may reroute calls for a few hours a day on one day, then shut off for several days so that its operations were neither predictable nor easy to detect.

"This is all done electronically, and it can be done in milliseconds," Coveney told me. "You then can isolate just the outcall calls and dump those calls to another outcall service. I'm sure that's how it was being done.

"The phone company had nothing to do with it. It was done in the—right inside the phone systems in each hotel."

With the call diversion going on in the switchboards of certain hotels, Coveney indicated, no amount of testing by the phone company of its own systems would uncover a problem.

"You could certainly do it inside of a switch in a hotel, yes," said Chip Falcon. But Falcon said he doubted Coveney was involved in any call diversion scheme for a couple of reasons.

"Charles had experience in bugging devices and that sort of thing," Falcon said, "But I don't think he had the level of sophistication to go program a PBX inside a hotel."

Falcon said Coveney came to him for assistance after Coveney's name surfaced as being a target of the alleged

Mob plot. Coveney wanted to know if a call diversion scheme was possible, and how, technically, it might have been accomplished. Falcon said Coveney's angst and anger over being named as a possible culprit in the suspected call diversion scheme seemed genuine. If Coveney's reaction was an act, it was an uncommonly good one.

"Charles should either win an Oscar—or he had significant anxiety over this," Falcon said.

But, even today, some people believe Sprint, the local phone company back then, was being hacked, even if it wasn't being done by Charles Coveney. And, after the outcall case was over, a high-profile hearing into call diversion would be held by the Nevada Public Utilities Commission that would reveal vulnerabilities in Sprint's phone system despite company officials insisting there was no evidence the system had been compromised. Experts would testify that gaps in security would allow someone to hack the system and take control of a phone line. But the question would be: just because calls *could* be diverted, did that mean calls *had* been diverted?

In October 1998, the alleged Mob associates looking to take over the Las Vegas call girl racket were convinced it *was* being done and they didn't particularly care *how* it was being done. They just wanted to grab the guy who was "making the phones funny" and make him work for them. That guy, they decided, rightly or wrongly, was Charles Coveney.

But finding Coveney would not be easy. Even his brother Bill, at the time, did not know where he was actually living. Bill told the FBI as much when agents came to him looking for Charles.

"When the FBI called me, I hadn't seen my brother in thirteen years," Bill Coveney said. "Because he disappeared. He moved out here and disappeared."

Charles Coveney's self-orchestrated disappearance and his careful covering of his own tracks would pose a major headache for any Mob soldiers looking for him. However, reputed Gambino crime family associate Mario Pugliese had promised undercover FBI informant Tony Nastasi that a couple of "aspirins" were being sent to take care of any headaches connected to the escort services.

One of those men literally bore the name nickname "Aspirins" as his Mob moniker. And, as federal agents would discover, Vinnie "Aspirins" Congiusti had developed a reputation of being just as skilled at causing headaches as he was at eliminating them.

Chapter Seven

Aspirins for a Headache

Las Vegas in the 1960s, '70s, and early '80s was very much a Mob town. It was an open city, so wiseguys flocked to Las Vegas from all across the country, but particularly from cities in the Midwest, like Detroit, Cleveland, Kansas City, and, of course, Chicago.

With the wiseguys came their Mob monikers, nicknames affixed to them by their associates or, in some cases, the press. One of the best known in Las Vegas was Chicago native Tony "The Ant" Spilotro, who ran a jewelry store/ fencing operation in Las Vegas, and whose criminal career was chronicled in the book and movie *Casino*. How he got the nickname "The Ant" is not completely clear. One veteran FBI agent claimed he'd given Spilotro the handle during a testy face-to-face meeting in which the agent called Spilotro a "pissant." At least one of Spilotro's surviving associates said the "The Ant" nickname was much more mundane and, simply, a short form of Anthony, Spilotro's first name.

New York's Vincent Congiusti had a Mob sobriquet, and there was little doubt about who gave it to him and what it meant. His organized crime associates dubbed him "Vinnie Aspirins" and it reflected his alleged vocation in the Mafia.

Retired FBI agent Dan DeSimone said he'll never forget the question he put to Congiusti about his moniker when DeSimone, while posing undercover as an escort service manager, found himself in a car with Vinnie and some other alleged organized crime associates.

"It was: Mr. Congiusti, how is that you happened to get the nickname 'The Aspirin?'"

DeSimone said there was a pause in the conversation that gave him second thoughts about what he'd just done.

"And we were in a vehicle and the vehicle went completely silent," DeSimone remembers. "And that one, two, three seconds kinda felt like it was 2-3 minutes. And for a moment there, I'm thinking, maybe I shouldn't have asked him. Is this gonna make him upset?

"And then, cool as day, calm as can be, he said, 'Kid, when the family has a headache, they call me. And I get rid of it.'"

"Vinnie Aspirins got the nickname by taking care of headaches for the Mob," echoes retired FBI agent Charles Maurer. "Whether it was through torture or murder or whatever, he was dispatched to take care of problems."

Maurer, who was the co-case agent for the FBI's escort service investigation, said Vinnie Aspirins was known for an unusual method of generating a headache in order to eliminate one.

"His reputation was that when questioning someone, he would drill a hole in their head or in their kneecap and torture them to make them tell him what he wanted to know."

When Vinnie Aspirins traveled, his suitcase might contain an electric drill. And his trip to Las Vegas was no exception. Federal agents ultimately found a battery-powered, cordless drill in his luggage.

Vinnie Aspirins was forty-nine-years old when he became involved in the outcall case. He had a raspy voice, a hang-dog facial expression, and looked like somebody central casting might send over if you were making a movie, needed somebody to play a generic Italian-uncle type, and Abe Vigoda wasn't available.

"Average size, average build," said former federal agent Dan DeSimone. "Not threatening to look at all."

Of course, looks can be deceiving.

Vinnie "Aspirins" Congiusti had drawn the attention of the FBI for some alleged rough stuff in Florida prior to flying to Las Vegas to assist in the outcall caper, though he hadn't been arrested in the Sunshine State. From a federal affidavit regarding the Florida case:

> Congiusti is currently the subject of an FBI investigation in Tampa, Florida. Congiusti is alleged to have attempted to extort $200,000 from a restaurant owner. During this extortion attempt, Congiusti held a gun to the restaurant owner's head. The extortion was thwarted because the restaurant owner was affiliated with the Bonanno LCN family.

In October of 1998, Vinnie Aspirins was dispatched to Las Vegas from Tampa, Florida, where federal agents believe he'd been helping Mario Pugliese with a cigarette smuggling operation out of the Bahamas. Traveling with Vinnie from Florida was a second, younger man named Anton Nelsen. Nelsen had picked up the nickname "Angel of Death," possibly because he was reputed to have worked as a mercenary. Nelsen was also suspected of being skilled in the art of arson and the use of explosives. He had reportedly demonstrated those skills on his own dentist's office.

"Anton Nelsen may have had a bad experience," former case agent Maurer said. "Anyway, he blew up the dentist's office. I'm not sure what the motive was, maybe he didn't like the dental work he got."

Vinnie Aspirins and Anton Nelsen were slated to meet up with Ken Byrnes, who was already on the ground in Las Vegas. Together, investigators would allege, the trio's job was to visit the major outcall service operators and deliver a message—with whatever force was necessary—on behalf of Mob-linked escort service owner Chris DeCarlo.

"And the choice they were going to have was either be killed or give up their outcall businesses to DeCarlo," said Maurer. "That was the mission for Vinnie Aspirins, Anton Nelsen, and Ken Byrnes."

Byrnes arrived in Las Vegas on October 1, 1998, nearly a week before Vinnie and Anton flew in. Byrnes had started putting together a list of names and addresses of the outcall owners who would need to be "talked to." He marked the locations of their homes and businesses on maps. DeCarlo had, at his disposal, a rental apartment and he gave Byrnes the keys. DeCarlo also provided one of his employees, a young man named Josh Snellings, to drive Byrnes around the city. For some reason, Byrnes would not or could not drive himself.

The FBI had gone to considerable lengths to keep track of Vinnie Aspirins, Anton Nelsen, and Ken Byrnes during their time in Las Vegas. The feds had obtained a court order to wiretap Byrnes' phone, and they were already consensually monitoring and recording the phone lines of their informant Tony Nastasi and undercover agent Dan DeSimone, in his role as "Danny Borelli," Nastasi's outcall service manager. Agents also got additional court permission to bug the hotel rooms of Nelsen and Vinnie Aspirins. All three of the alleged Mob associates were eventually put under twenty-four-hour surveillance, a costly proposition for the Las Vegas FBI office in terms of manpower.

But the seemingly sinister dialogue being captured by the bugs and the wiretaps had agents on edge, and the extraordinary effort to keep constant tabs on the suspects was deemed necessary. For example, in one wiretapped conversation between Nastasi and Byrnes, Byrnes nonchalantly discusses the idea of having Vinnie put his power tools to work on the top escort service owner in Las

Vegas as a way of sending a message to the other service owners.

"Vinnie's idea, and I discussed it with him yesterday, is to maybe 'aspirinize' the one guy on top and then put everybody else in line," Byrnes said on the surreptitiously made recording. "I don't know if that's the right way to go. I mean, I don't know how much publicity that would bring."

Later, during the same wiretapped recording, Byrnes asks rhetorically how much heat it would generate if the top tier of Las Vegas outcall service owners were suddenly eliminated.

"If, say, all five of them were to sort of like, you know, go away. And the guys taking their place would then be put in line. How much of a fucking—how much of a ripple effect would that create?

"I just don't know how to play it yet. I've got four days to figure it out, how to play this fucking thing."

Byrnes' talk of "aspirinizing" one outcall service owner and making the five top players "go away" was elevating the concern of FBI agents listening to the wiretaps. Also, Byrnes mentioning that he had four days to sort things out pointed out the fact that a clock was ticking. Something drastic could very well happen in the next four days, and agents had to be ready for it.

On October 7, 1998, just before 9:00 a.m., Vinnie and Anton arrived in Las Vegas on a flight from Tampa. Undercover surveillance agents from the FBI were at the airport and watching their every move.

From the search warrant affidavit in that case:

> *Also, during the morning of October 7, 1998, CW-1 (Nastasi) telephonically contacted Byrnes. Byrnes advised he was in the company of Vinnie and the other individual from Tampa. Byrnes put Congiusti on the telephone with CW-1. Congiusti advised CW-1 that they expect to make contact with outcall service*

*operators and he expects that one of them
will "go bang." CW-1 believes this means
that Congiusti and the others plan to blow up
someone's office. CW-1 stated that Pugliesi
told him on a previous occasion that Vinnie's
partner blew up his dentist's office because he
was angry with the dentist.*

*Congiusti, Nelsen, and Byrnes were under
physical surveillance by FBI agents during
October 7, 1998, and October 8, 1998. During
this time period Congiusti, Nelsen, and Byrnes
were observed to meet with Christiano DeCarlo
on at least five occasions.*

*Two of the meetings occurred at DeCarlo's
place of business and one occurred in a
hotel room at the Alexis Park Resort Hotel,
Las Vegas, Nevada. The meeting at the hotel
included the above four individuals and
another unknown individual. The unknown
individual was observed carrying a suitcase
into the hotel room and leaving without it.*

*During a physical surveillance on October
7, 1998, Congiusti, Nelsen, and Byrnes were
observed in the above described 1998 Ford
Expedition in the vicinity of 900 East Karen
Avenue, Las Vegas, Nevada. This address is the
business address of Richard Soranno.*

While the suspects were out of their rooms checking the
addresses of the local outcall service owners, FBI agents
were checking out the suspects' rooms. Agents discovered
the rooms had been rented by DeCarlo and had a departure
date of October 10. Now, agents not only knew a clock was
ticking, but they also knew how much time was left on it.

Whatever the alleged Mob associates planned to do, they would likely try to get it done before October 10.

But, even before Byrnes, Nelsen, and Vinnie Aspirins landed in Las Vegas, local FBI agents had gotten wind of yet another alleged plot by Chris DeCarlo to kill an outcall service owner, this time using members of a criminal organization far different from the Mafia.

The FBI office in Los Angeles had received a tip from one of its confidential informants that DeCarlo had reached out to two members of the Rollin '60s Crips street gang. The pair of L.A. gang bangers had been hired, according to the informant, to whack a Las Vegas outcall service owner who supposedly had connections with a Mafia family in Philadelphia.

The FBI informant was later identified as Kenny "Kenji" Gallo, a Japanese-Italian former Mob associate who "flipped" for the feds and provided FBI agents with inside information about the L.A. Mafia. In a book about his own exploits with organized crime and how he turned his life around, Gallo talks about how DeCarlo met the two gang bangers at a sleazy, now-defunct topless bar in Orange County, California, called Captain Cream's. The bar was near a shop where Gallo once peddled pornography.

According to Gallo, the two Crips, who went by the nicknames "Crazy Larry" and "Ikon," were introduced to DeCarlo by a paralegal in a Las Vegas law office who was originally from Southern California. Gallo said he thought Crazy Larry and Ikon might rob DeCarlo, thinking he was just a young goomba with a high-end watch strapped around his wrist, but the gang bangers ended up going to work for the young escort service owner. Gallo said DeCarlo dropped a number of names as organized crime references during the meeting at the topless bar, names which, to Gallo's surprise, actually checked out. Gallo, for his part, made DeCarlo aware of his own connections to the L.A. Mafia, and told DeCarlo to call on him if he ever needed anything. Gallo soon learned that Crazy Larry and Ikon had been hired by DeCarlo to get rid of that rival escort service owner in Las Vegas who had connections to the Philadelphia crime family.

Gallo said he immediately informed his FBI handlers, but word of the plot didn't reach Las Vegas FBI agents until September 9, even though the gangsters left L.A. for Las Vegas on September 1.

The reason for the delay, said Gallo: "Bureaucracy. The FBI out of L.A. wasn't coordinating the information. I'm like, dude, these guys have guns. They're going.

"The FBI has been really good to me, but sometimes they did a lot of incompetent things. This was one of those things."

Fortunately, the Las Vegas FBI was able to pick up the trail of the alleged hitmen, in part because agents knew who the Crips were targeting and where the target lived and worked.

According to court documents filed in the case, Crazy Larry and Ikon conducted extensive surveillance of the Philadelphia-linked outcall owner but were unable to find an opportunity to kill him.

During the course of their activities in Las Vegas, the two L.A. Crips were involved in a hit and run car accident. Here's how Gallo described what happened in his own book, *Breakshot*:

> *One of DeCarlo's murder plots self-destructed of its own accord. In the process of looking for their target from Philadelphia, the smoked-out and paranoid Crazy Larry and Ikon crashed their pickup truck on the Las Vegas Strip. Panicking that the cops would soon arrive at the scene of the wreck, the two tripping Crips spun the truck back into traffic and fled. It all happened so fast that the FBI cars trailing*

their truck lost sight of Crazy Larry and Ikon instantly. They were never caught.

Although the pair of alleged hitmen got away, the FBI in Los Angeles received information from Gallo that at least one of them was planning to travel back to Las Vegas and complete the job that had been aborted. The gangster told Gallo he had four guns, a silencer, and body armor.

The Las Vegas FBI warned the targeted outcall service owner about the threat on his life and advised him to leave town for a week or two. Agents believe that's exactly what he did. The alleged hitmen never got close to him.

Why DeCarlo would single out a particular outcall service owner for murder and solicit street gangsters for a hit was never fully explained. But, the FBI's decision to warn the victim would surface as a point of controversy when the investigation was over, because agents in Las Vegas did not also warn outcall mavens Richard Soranno and Frank Bartello about the plot that was developing with them as targets.

Retired agent Charles Maurer said the FBI didn't believe a warning was necessary in the cases of Soranno and Bartello, because agents had been monitoring the communications and travel plans of suspected Mob enforcers Byrnes, Nelsen, and Vinnie Aspirins. All three were under the constant eye of undercover federal agents from the moment they set foot in Clark County, Nevada. Agents believed they'd be able to step in before any of the alleged Mob associates could get close enough to harm Soranno and Bartello.

"They had no idea of any of the plots against them. We didn't tell them beforehand because we didn't want to compromise any of the investigation," Maurer said. "Plus, we felt we had one hundred percent control of the situation; we had surveillance on Bartello, surveillance on Soranno, and surveillance on the subjects involved. We were confident nothing could happen to Bartello or Soranno during that period."

It's true that agents eventually did warn Charles Coveney that he was being targeted, but they were seeking his cooperation. Even then, agents were not able to sit down and talk with him until the day, or a few days, before the outcall investigation came to a climax.

Finding Coveney would be a key task for the trio sent to tip the tables of the Las Vegas escort game in favor of the Mob-linked Chris DeCarlo. But Coveney's importance, and his role in the overall plan to take control of sex services in Las Vegas, might also prove to be a key point of friction among the suspected Mob associates. As investigators watched and listened, that friction seemed to smolder until it reached a point where two of the alleged Mob enforcers would be caught on a hidden mike talking about arranging for the third to have an untimely, and potentially fatal, "accident."

Chapter Eight

Chasing Coveney

On October 5, 1998, while having lunch in New York City with undercover FBI informant Tony Nastasi, reputed Gambino crime family associate Mario Pugliesi dropped the name that would add a new dimension to the FBI's investigation of escort services in Las Vegas. Nastasi, also known to federal agents as confidential witness number one (CW-1), was recording the conversation with a body-worn audio recorder. From the search warrant affidavit in the case:

> *On or about October 5, 1998, Pugliesi told CW-1 that in addition to the outcall business operators targeted, he has targeted an individual named Charles Coveney. Pugliesi said that Coveney is a computer expert who currently works for Soranno. Coveney has contacts in the Sprint Telephone Company and is able to have telephone calls diverted from one number to another. Pugliesi expects to persuade Coveney to leave Soranno and assist DeCarlo in his outcall business by diverting telephone calls to DeCarlo.*

Las Vegas agents recognized the name Soranno as one of the top operators of outcall entertainment services in the city. But Coveney's name had not been mentioned before now. Up until this point, there had been general talk about telephone calls being diverted away from Mob-connected escort services. But this meeting marked the first time a name had been attached as a mastermind to the call diversion scheme.

"It was rumored he had done that kind of work for the Mob before," said former agent Maurer. "Ken Byrnes came up with that name."

Byrnes passed the name on to Pugliese, who, in turn, mentioned it to Nastasi.

"Mario Pugliese believed Charles Coveney worked for Soranno and was diverting calls into Soranno's business," Maurer said. "And he told the cooperating witness as much. They were searching for Coveney originally because they wanted him to work for Chris DeCarlo instead of Richard Soranno and divert calls into DeCarlo's business— instead of Soranno's—from the others."

And what might happen to Coveney if he refused to cooperate with the suspected wiseguys should they catch up with him?

"They were going to kill him if he didn't agree to work for them," Maurer opines.

At the time Pugliese identified Coveney as the phone call diversion expert, Coveney's name was new to Las Vegas FBI agents. And though it might seem unlikely that they would be unaware of Coveney's past work as a law-enforcement informant, in the mid-1990s the amount of information available on the internet was not nearly as vast as it is today. There was a secure FBI database of informants that agents could access to make sure they didn't accidentally interfere with another office's case, but Maurer said he had no reason at the time to run Coveney's name through it. Despite the fact that Coveney had been an FBI informant in New York and Florida in the late '70s, Las Vegas agents initially weren't familiar with his work and may have been uncertain he had the requisite skills to intercept and redirect phone calls.

But it seems clear the guys sent by reputed Mob associate Mario Pugliese were of the opinion Coveney was the man "making the phones funny" and they had Coveney squarely in their sights. FBI agents, just as they had done with outcall owners Bartello and Soranno, would need to find Coveney, either to put him under protective surveillance or to warn him he was a target. Also, if Coveney really had any knowledge about how the call diversion scheme worked, agents might make a deal with the computer expert to gain his cooperation.

So, the feds and the suspected wiseguys started looking for Coveney. It wouldn't be a cakewalk for the FBI, and it would be doubly difficult for the conspirators in the outcall case. The FBI's efforts would ultimately lead to the meeting between agents and Coveney at the pancake house on East Charleston Boulevard just before the case came to a head. The reputed wiseguys would never get near Coveney.

Late in the case, Ken Byrnes would be captured on a monitored phone line telling Tony Nastasi of his frustration—and apparent grudging admiration—for the way Coveney had managed to melt into his surroundings.

"This is our guy, Tony, Coveney," Byrnes said on the covertly made recording. "We're trying to snatch Coveney—can't get a hold of the motherfucker. He hides so well. We found fourteen different addresses for the cocksucker. Can you believe it? Fourteen different addresses."

It's not surprising the suspects might have checked out fourteen addresses for Coveney and still came up empty, when you consider where much of their information was coming from. In fact, the source of some of their data was almost comical. In a roundabout way, the information—a lot of it anyway—was coming indirectly from the FBI. Kenji Gallo had offered Chris DeCarlo use of his Mob connections during DeCarlo's California visit. Once DeCarlo was back in Vegas, he reached out to Gallo. Gallo, in his capacity as an informant for the L.A. FBI office, was also the person named as confidential witness number two (CW-2) in the Vegas outcall case.

From the search warrant affidavit:

> *CW-2 on October 8, 1998, had a telephone call with DeCarlo ... DeCarlo indicated it was essential to find the address for Coveney. DeCarlo explained that three people were in from Tampa and if they did not complete their plans, they would come back at a later time.*

"I had a guy who worked at LexisNexis," Gallo remembers. "So, he had an unlimited account with P search, or people search.

"I got Coveney's phone number. And from that phone number I got an address. Now, I don't know if that address was right or wrong, but the FBI gave me (a fake) one to give 'em."

Gallo said he worked closely with his L.A. FBI handlers to give the suspected Mob associates in Las Vegas stale or out-of-date information that would seem legit but would be otherwise useless.

"When you look at old property records, utility searches—that kind of thing—you can get dead ones, where the guy used to be.

"I did the real search, and I showed the other guys that I did the search, but I didn't give 'em the real information," Gallo said.

The bogus location data about Coveney that Gallo was supplying to DeCarlo may have had the purported wiseguys scurrying all over Vegas with little chance of actually finding their target. At the same time, knowing the locations in advance where the suspects would be searching would have, in theory, made it that much easier for the FBI to keep tabs on them. It appeared to be a wild goose chase orchestrated by—and for the benefit of—federal agents.

But just because Coveney had become a priority, it didn't mean the crew sent by Pugliese was abandoning its original plan to "bang some heads" to get the Las Vegas outcall operators in line. The Mob-linked men were able to develop their own information from public records about the locations of the various outcall offices and the houses owned by people like Soranno and Bartello.

In one wiretapped conversation between Byrnes and Nastasi, intercepted by federal agents, Byrnes noted that Soranno's house looked less like something he'd associate with a successful sex-industry entrepreneur than the home of somebody "working part time at Taco Bell."

In some of the wiretapped conversations, Coveney's name is used openly, but the conspirators also started using what appears to be coded language to describe the computer expert. Coveney is referred to as "the piano man," an apparent reference to Coveney's genius with a keyboard. Mafia families were called "law firms" and "members" of a family were referred to as "lawyers" for those firms.

In a phone call between Byrnes and DeCarlo, intercepted late in the case by the FBI, Vinnie Aspirins rebuked Byrnes for not using a code word and then did the same thing himself:

> Byrnes: *Josh had mentioned that Coveney was, was—*
>
> Vinnie Aspirins (in the background): *Stop using his motherfucking name.*
>
> Byrnes: *Ok, the "piano man" was, was, uh ... on the lam or hiding because someone was after him...*

Here, someone in the background can be heard joking (presumably) that they'll shoot Byrnes if he uses Coveney's name again.

"Go ahead, please, do me a favor. Shoot me!" Byrnes jokes back. Then he goes on with his story about Coveney supposedly being on the lam.

> Byrnes: *That he was basically lamb-chopping it because he had done the wrong thing by some people like we know down in Philadelphia. He used the "m" word, ok? So, ask Josh if that was Philadelphia or not, because if it is, we have some people we can start making some calls right now about that.*
>
> DeCarlo: *It was Philadelphia, I can tell you that right now.*
>
> Byrnes: *It was?*
>
> DeCarlo: *Yeah.*
>
> Byrnes (to Vinnie Aspirins): *Vinnie, it was Philadelphia, so why don't we just ...*
>
> Vinnie Aspirins (interrupting): *Yeah, but we need a name, we need a family, a law firm –*
>
> DeCarlo: *Lombardo.*

It is unknown whether or not the talk of a "family" or "law firm" from Philadelphia was connected to the earlier incident involving the Rollin 60's and the Philly-linked outcall service owner. The call in which the "Lombardo" name first surfaced came about a month after the gangbangers from L.A. aborted their mission in Las Vegas.

The "piano man" code name for Coveney pops up in another phone conversation, captured on tape by federal agents. Chris DeCarlo tells Anton Nelsen what he's discovered through his own sources of information, apparently independent of what was coming from Kenji Gallo:

> DeCarlo: *Anton, one of the places of employment on the piano man came up as*

Escobedo and Associates. Eddie Escobedo as the owner. They cross referenced that name and the address of his workplace with the addresses with the Clark County Business Department, with all the escort service owners. It came up the same one. There's an Eddie Escobedo and Associates with an outcall entertainer's license — which is the same thing as what we do: escorts. That's the same thing that came up underneath Coveney.

Anton Nelsen: *That's his address?*

DeCarlo: *Same one. So, they have to be running it out of there. This is 845 N. Eastern Avenue.*

In fact, 845 N. Eastern Avenue *was* owned by Escobedo, and Escobedo's company, Escobedo and Associates, did have a "professional promoter" license with Clark County dating as far back as 1989. But county officials say that license could not have been used legally to dispatch escorts or outcall entertainers. According to county business licensing records, the "promoter" license was obtained to promote Latin dancing, and that license was issued for an office at 760 N. Eastern Avenue. The building at 845 N. Eastern was small, old, and, at that time, the only licensed business there was a lawn maintenance firm.

In any event, Chris DeCarlo had discovered, possibly under a false assumption, a real connection between Coveney and Escobedo. And there's evidence DeCarlo also had access to information from Binion's Horseshoe as well. In a phone call between DeCarlo and Byrnes secretly recorded by the FBI, DeCarlo directed Byrnes to check out a business address for Coveney in downtown Las Vegas on Las Vegas Boulevard.

"Coveney's address is the same as Renie and Raymond Computers," DeCarlo said. "That is the Manpower Building. Same address as they have in the Horseshoe computer."

Indeed, Coveney did spend time at the Manpower Building downtown where he was not known as the "piano man" but as "Charlie the Chooch." Coveney used the Renie and Raymond computer office as a sort of informal clubhouse to hang out and network with other techies.

"He needed some place to fiddle around with his computer equipment," said David Raymond, former partner in Renie and Raymond Computers.

Thus, the Manpower Building was not Coveney's real home. Nonetheless, DeCarlo and company had discovered through their own sources, perhaps accidentally, very real connections between Coveney, Binion's Horseshoe, and Eddie Escobedo.

It's not clear from court records in the case whether the feds ever found out where Coveney was actually living. The suspects in the case certainly didn't.

"I don't remember *not* knowing where he lived," said Maurer. But Maurer also confirms that the only time he met Coveney was during the meeting at the pancake house on East Charleston Boulevard shortly before the end of the investigation, and that meeting was arranged by telephone, not through a face-to-face encounter at Coveney's home. Mauer's former co-case agent, Jerry Hanford, said he never did find out where Coveney was living at the time.

It's possible, as Coveney had told Mike Bindrup, the mysterious computer programmer's residence was a Horseshoe Hotel room that—to put it in telephone terms Coveney would probably appreciate—had an "unlisted number." Coveney could easily have made sure a false home address was stored in the computer used by the Horseshoe to keep track of employee or guest information.

Wherever he was living, Coveney's ability to stay hidden was possibly helping to create a rift among the alleged Mob associates attempting the hostile takeover. Ken Byrnes was on one side of the schism while Anton Nelsen and Vinnie Aspirins were on the other. According to court records, it appeared that Byrnes was focused on snatching Coveney and getting him to use his computer skills to steal business away from the Mob's rivals, while Nelsen and Aspirins favored the time-honored strategy of grabbing the top outcall service owners and threatening them with bodily harm unless they capitulated.

From the search warrant application:

> *On October 9, 1998, in the early morning, Congiusti and Nelsen discussed the fact that they needed to revisit some of the locations they had previously observed but that Byrnes had the map. On October 9, 1998, 12:59 a.m., a conversation was intercepted between Congiusti and Nelsen in Room 1860 at the Alexis Park Hotel. During the conversation the men commented that they wanted a limo to deliver them to a location. A comment was made that they were not going to hurt someone at the location but they were going to make him think so.*

> *Congiusti said it was too bad Mario (Pugliesi) told the "kid" (DeCarlo) that they had a "badge" (member of the LCN) because now they had to go through with it. They discussed trying to find a house in Northwest Las Vegas at 6:00 a.m. in the morning and busting down the door. They made the comment that they were going to get the "B guy."*

> *They said that Kenny (Byrnes) was stuck on the Coveney deal. They commented that Byrnes was stupid and not cautious.*

The observation by Nelsen and Vinnie Aspirins that Ken Byrnes was "stupid and not cautious," is from one of several conversations captured by hidden FBI listening devices in which Nelsen and Aspirins reveal their apparent displeasure with Byrnes.

In one recording, Nelsen raises the possibility that Byrnes might "roll" to the feds, possibly because of the IRS money laundering operation in which Byrnes had been implicated, but not yet indicted.

"What do you think about Kenny?" Nelsen asked Aspirins.

"I think he's a fucking psychotic," Aspirins replied. "Why?"

"Other than that?"

"He's got a big fucking mouth," Aspirins responded.

"He's still got a lot of shit hanging over his head," Nelsen noted.

"Well, he makes it sound a lot worse than what it is, Anton," Aspirins said. "This is an old game from running the credit cards through a thing out here. Why the fuck would they be giving him twenty years (for that)? He's full of shit."

"Yeah, but I've seen guys roll for less than that," Nelsen observed.

Nelsen and Aspirins are captured on one of the hotel room bugs talking about "doing" Byrnes when their Las Vegas assignment is over.

"After we do this piece of work, should we do Kenny, too?" Aspirins asked.

"Yeah," Nelsen replied.

"It's ok by me, "Aspirins said. "He pisses me off more than he pleases me."

The tough talk gets even tougher in another secretly recorded conversation.

"Kenny makes me nervous," Nelsen said to Aspirins.

"You wanna go out shooting, again?" Aspirins asked. "Have an accident? You reach for a weapon and the guy says, 'diplomatic immunity.' And I'll just yell out 'accidental discharge!'"

It might have been hard for an FBI agent monitoring these conversations to discern whether the apparent talk of offing Ken Byrnes was just two tough guys letting off steam, bullshitting one another, or the prelude to an actual hit. But a diligent FBI agent, listening to these conversations, could easily see it as an indication of potentially deadly rancor and/or suspicion developing among the alleged Mob associates.

While Anton Nelsen and Vinnie Aspirins were bad-mouthing Byrnes to each other, Byrnes was trash-talking Aspirins behind his back in phone conversations with Mario Pugliese. Byrnes said Aspirins seemed more interested in finding new dining locations in Las Vegas than locating the outcall owners and putting them all in line.

"I tell ya, he's a prick," said Byrnes in one intercepted conversation. But Byrnes did express admiration for Nelsen, referencing an apparent earlier trip to a shooting range or deserted location for target practice.

"He's good with the tools, right?" Pugliese inquired about Nelsen.

"Yeah, like 'The Jackal,'" Byrnes replied. "He's good with the tools. Very, very much so. He's a marksman. He's a good shot."

"Not the other guy (Aspirins)," said Pugliese.

"No," Byrnes laughed.

"The other guy can't see," Pugliese said, a reference to the fact that Aspirins' eyesight was so poor he was legally blind. "He needs, like, a cannon."

Byrnes told Pugliese that Aspirins seemed content driving around, surveilling the outcall offices, hoping, possibly, to catch the owners going in or out while Byrnes favored a more direct approach. He wanted to go into the buildings and force a sit-down with the outcall owners about Coveney and the call diversion.

Pugliese seemed to agree Aspirins was playing it too cautiously. He noted that risk is part of their thing.

"If you don't wanna do this and you don't wanna do that—if you don't wanna get into trouble, then maybe you should sell popcorn in a movie house," Pugliese said.

The elder Mob associate also questioned what the Tampa guys have been doing with all their time in Vegas. Pugliese, like Byrnes, seemed to think finding Coveney should be job one.

"If all you have to do is go after one guy, it's a shame they didn't grab him already."

"I mean, what do they want?" Pugliese asked rhetorically. "This guy to surrender to them? Go do your job. Why is that so hard? They wanted a car. They got a drill. What do they do all day?"

"Not a whole lot," Byrnes answered.

To which Pugliese quipped: "What do ya got the drill for? What are you gonna do, put up cabinets?"

In fact, the cordless drill would not be used to assemble cabinets, but it would play a significant role in events that were shortly to unfold. That would be October 9, 1998, scheduled to be the last full day for the crew in Las Vegas and, despite the possible discord and frayed relationships among the suspected wiseguys, they did seem to agree on one thing: if they couldn't grab Coveney, putting pressure on somebody who knew where he was hiding would be the next best thing. According to federal investigators, Phil Bunin, a self-described Las Vegas media consultant who had contacts in the escort industry, was one man the suspected Mob enforcers would eventually try to pry Coveney's location out of.

Byrnes and Pugliese were caught on tape talking about "Phil" shortly before Bunin was summoned to DeCarlo's office for questioning.

"So, we'll see what happens now with Phil," Pugliese said. "Then the next thing they're gonna do (Aspirins, Nelsen) is plan where they're going to eat tonight."

"Yeah, I know," said Byrnes. "That's the big thing all the time, you know, for the Aspirin. Not getting this thing resolved like I wanna resolve it."

"Maybe it's too much to do in two days," Pugliese observed. But Byrnes was adamant that Aspirins' laid-back approach had kept the plan from moving forward.

"There's too much and then there's nothing," Byrnes said. "There's a difference. Riding around looking at people's houses and buildings does not constitute a search."

Byrnes expressed similar sentiments in a call to DeCarlo, also secretly recorded by the FBI.

"I'm becoming very frustrated at the lack of forward movement," Byrnes told DeCarlo. "You don't know me well enough to know that when I have a task that I always, always, always complete it. I always stick to my word. And so far, this has become like hitting my head against the wall."

DeCarlo was philosophical and seemed to be expressing hope they would get the answers they were looking for—including Coveney's location—once they had a chance to talk to Phil.

"You think he's looking for information around town?" DeCarlo asked.

"Yes," said Byrnes. "Unless I miss my guess, he will, in fact, plug himself in one way or the other. If he doesn't have answers tomorrow, he will have them in the near future. Especially with his own ass on the chopping block."

As Byrnes predicted, the next day found all of the Vegas crew, including DeCarlo, at DeCarlo's office with Phil Bunin on the hot seat.

What none of the players knew was that a contingent of undercover FBI agents would be nearby, monitoring what happened, ready to pounce should the questioning of Bunin change from a grilling to a drilling.

Chapter Nine

Takedown

"I've got to talk quietly because they're in next door; they're working on some guy."

Those chilling words, which began this book, marked the beginning of the end for the alleged Mafia plot to take control of Las Vegas escort services in October 1998. Ken Byrnes was in an office adjacent to the office of escort service owner Chris DeCarlo. At some point, Byrnes got on a phone with Tony Nastasi, the escort service owner who pretended to be allied with DeCarlo, and Byrnes described what was supposedly the interrogation of Las Vegas media man Phil Bunin by DeCarlo, Anton Nelsen, and Vinnie "Aspirins" Congiusti.

The suspected Mob associates were trying to find out, according to federal investigators, what Bunin knew about Charles Coveney, the computer expert they believed was working for a rival escort service and hacking the phone system to intercept calls meant for other services, including DeCarlo's. Byrnes was giving Tony Nastasi a blow-by-blow description of the alleged grilling, not realizing Nastasi was an FBI informant, and the phone call was being monitored and recorded.

"We think we have an 'in' with this guy that knows a little bit more than he says and they're—how shall we say—persuading him," Byrnes told Nastasi.

"Now, this guy, is he one of the principals or is this a guy that makes the phones funny?" Nastasi asked.

"That guy that makes the phones funny?" Byrnes replied, "We looked everywhere, and we cannot dig this cocksucker up. You name it, and we can't find him. But we think we can get to him through this guy."

Nastasi asked an obvious question, to find out where all this is going.

"What are we gonna have to do, pay this guy or–"

"No, no, no, no, no, no, no, no," Byrnes laughed. "There's other ways to motivate people. Aspirin brought his power tools."

There's a pause in the conversation, then this:

"I don't believe it," said Byrnes.

"What?"

"I can hear the drill bit going next door," Byrnes said. "The cordless drill. I don't hear any screams, though. Probably just putting it next to his head."

Nastasi urged caution.

"Yeah, you don't wanna—you're gonna have a package to get rid of if something goes wrong."

"Exactly," said Byrnes, laughing.

At this point Nastasi started to beg off from the conversation. He wasn't sure if the FBI was listening to the conversation real-time and, if not, he needed to alert his handlers to what was going on. But before Nastasi ended the call, Byrnes made the point that one of the top outcall service owners may soon get a visit from Vinnie and his drill.

"They're gonna have to do an 'aspirin' situation with one of these guys, to send a message. You know that."

As it turns out, the FBI was monitoring the Nastasi-Byrnes phone call in real time, and when agents who were listening in heard the things Byrnes was saying, they immediately radioed the team of agents hidden outside DeCarlo's office. The hair-raising remarks from Byrnes to Nastasi left agents no choice but to charge in and arrest all the Vegas conspirators before anything bad happened to Phil Bunin.

"And when they started talking about the drill, we were out in the parking lot and decided to hit the place at that point," said retired agent Charles Maurer.

"We pulled up in front of the office where they were," said retired co-case agent Jerry Hanford. "We wanted to do this as quickly as possible. We didn't want this guy getting killed or drilled or anything else."

When agents burst through the door, Anton Nelsen had a gun and two knives on his person, DeCarlo had a pistol on a desk within arm's reach and Vinnie Aspirins was carrying a switchblade knife.

Agents got a warrant to search DeCarlo's office as well as the Ford Expedition that Josh Snellings had been using to squire the conspirators around in. Among other things, they found a black bag containing rope, duct tape, two boxes of ammunition, a .357 magnum revolver, three pairs of binoculars, leather gloves, a .45 caliber handgun, walkie-talkies, a leather sap, a silencer, carburetor cleaner, which agents suspected was for use in a fire bomb, and, of course, Vinnie Aspirins' cordless drill.

"You don't normally take these things on vacation," Jerry Hanford noted.

The drill was found inside Vinnie Aspirins' luggage, which was still in the crew's Ford Expedition at the time, and not in DeCarlo's office. Whatever Byrnes heard while on the phone with Nastasi—if anything—was not that drill. Still, based on Byrnes' remarks, agents felt they had little choice but to rush in and make their arrests.

It was a premature climax to an investigation that had been unfolding for a year but had yet to produce definitive evidence of corruption by county law enforcement officials or call diversion by computer hackers.

"Well, we wanted to keep the case going in order to find out if we could actually fix the cooperating witness' case with the D.A.'s office and whether we would ever get warned when the Metro vice squad set up a sting," said former agent Maurer. "So, we wanted to keep the case going as long as we could, but in this instance, we had to act."

However, even if Phil Bunin hadn't been summoned to DeCarlo's office to face an interrogation by Vinnie Aspirins and crew, agents were considering arresting the suspected wiseguys later that day anyway, to keep them from flying back to their respective homes in New Jersey and Florida. Their fear was that the crew might return to Las Vegas at a later date, without being detected, to complete the unfinished business of "aspirinizing" outcall mavens like Richard Soranno and Frank Bartello.

"At that point, we were in control. If they come back, they could drive back by car and we might not know they're in town. They might harm either one of these people," Maurer said. "So, we knew we had to do something soon, regardless. But the fact that Bunin was in the office, and we had information that he was being tortured, we acted right away."

Bunin was unharmed and his head was intact. Bunin told the agents he said whatever DeCarlo and the rest of the crew wanted to hear in order to get out of the office.

In addition to wanting to know where Coveney was, Bunin said, DeCarlo demanded that Bunin pay him either twelve or twenty thousand dollars for work an acquaintance of Bunin's was supposed to have performed on DeCarlo's computers but didn't. DeCarlo, Nelsen, Byrnes, Snelling, and Vinnie Aspirins were all arrested on the spot. A judge ordered them held in jail pending trial, as they were determined to be a danger to the community. Not long after the arrests, the men were all indicted by a federal grand jury in Las Vegas on charges of interference with commerce by threat of violence, interstate travel in aid of racketeering, conspiracy, and possessing a firearm during a crime of violence.

When the charges were made public, no one was more surprised than outcall service owners Richard Soranno and Frank Bartello, who discovered to their chagrin, they'd been targets of an alleged Mob plot.

"Of course, I'm scared. I'm terrified," Soranno said, in an October 15, 1998, story in the *Las Vegas Sun.*

"I could go out, start my car and get blown up like some hood. But what am I going to do? I got over 100 people who work for me. I've got responsibilities. I've got nowhere to go."

As for not being warned he was being stalked by suspected Mob associates, Soranno told the *Sun:*

"I'm mad at the FBI. Shouldn't their proactive measures include getting to the victims? I think they put themselves first and looked at me as just a statistic."

Retired agent Maurer said both Soranno and Barello resented the fact they weren't warned about the plot before the plotters were arrested.

Maurer said he understands the outcall owners' ire. But he said it was necessary to keep the investigation a secret until its conclusion, and agents were confident they had things under control because the suspects and the outcall owners were all under constant physical surveillance.

"I told them we had everything covered 100% in our opinion, and no harm would have come to them," Maurer said. "But, naturally, they were upset at that."

Although the majority of the conspirators were arrested on October 9, 1998, in DeCarlo's office, there was one key player still outstanding: Mario Pugliese, aka Mario Stefano. Pugliese was in New York when the bust went down, but it didn't take him long to hear about it.

According to investigators, Pugliese quickly came to the conclusion there was a snitch somewhere in their midst, but apparently his suspicions about who it might be were woefully inaccurate. Nowhere is this fact more evident than in the wiretapped phone conversation Pugliese had with

"Danny," the man he thought was Nastasi's escort service manager but was actually undercover FBI agent Daniel DeSimone. During that conversation, according to court records, Pugliese tells the undercover agent he's sending two more guys to Las Vegas, one from Tampa and another from Cincinnati, to finish the job started by Vinnie Aspirins and, if the informant is found, to whack him. The call from Pugliese came not long after the arrests in Las Vegas and included a warning from Pugliese to DeSimone to stay away from DeCarlo's office in order to avoid getting arrested himself.

"He didn't use the term, 'you're with me now,' but he basically said, 'Come on back to New York and let's get into some cigarette smuggling coming up from the south," DeSimone recalls. "And that was kinda to be the next chapter."

DeSimone said there was thought given to keeping the undercover operation going and nab Mario Pugliese, aka Stefano, in the middle of the cigarette smuggling scheme. But government lawyers took a close look at the outcall case and determined there was sufficient evidence to charge Mario in that operation, so there was no need to continue the undercover investigation to include the cigarette smuggling. That left one final duty for Dan DeSimone to perform as supposed outcall service manager Danny Borelli.

"My role as the undercover agent was to lure—or meet up with—Mario Stefano for lunch, and the FBI would come in soon after lunch began and arrest Mario."

DeSimone made arrangements to meet Pugliese and Tony Nastasi for lunch at Pete's Tavern at 18th and Irving Place in New York, said to be the oldest bar in Manhattan. Pugliese is oblivious to the fact that Nastasi and "Danny" are working for the FBI. The three men are about to break bread when an FBI arrest team storms in.

Nastasi and DeSimone were expecting the bust.

In his Coast-to-Coast AM radio interview, Nastasi described the raid in terms that imply a certain Keystone Cops quality about it, since he said the officers initially missed the booth Nastasi, DeSimone, and Pugliese were sitting in.

"The FBI, they were all suited-up, they looked like Ninja Turtles, they had all their gear on," Nastasi said. "And they came running in. And they ran right by us, to the back of the place. There was about seven of them," Nastasi said.

"And finally, they come running back. And then they go through the motions, we're both under arrest, and they take us away."

DeSimone's recollection of the raid differs somewhat from Nastasi's, and DeSimone said Nastasi may have misinterpreted the actions of the arresting agents because Nastasi is not a trained law enforcement officer. DeSimone said the agents who went past the table where Pugliese and Nastasi were sitting probably did so to make sure various entrances to the tavern were covered and that none of the officers ended up in each other's potential line of fire.

DeSimone had excused himself from the table where Nastasi and Pugliese were sitting shortly before the bust, after first making sure one of the large windows at Pete's Tavern was open. When the arrest team started to take Nastasi and Pugliese into custody, DeSimone darted out through the open window in what appeared to be an "escape."

"The FBI had my picture, knew who I was, that I was one of them still undercover, and that they would quote, allow me to escape."

Of course, it was all for show. After Nastasi and Pugliese were arrested, the men were separated and the informant immediately uncuffed once the two were out of sight of each other. By this time, the "escaped" Daniel DeSimone was in the welcome company of members of the arrest team and on his way to be debriefed by fellow federal agents at the New York FBI office.

It's only later, after Nastasi and DeSimone are not charged and lawyers for the defendants start getting the paperwork on the case, that Pugliese and the others realize they've been doing business with a cooperating witness for the FBI and an actual undercover agent.

One of the more interesting documents filed in the court record by defense lawyers concerned Vinnie Aspirins. Mario Pugliese had joked about Aspirins' eyesight in one of the phone conversations intercepted by federal agents, and a financial affidavit Vinnie filed with the court stated that he was, in fact, legally blind. This prompted a TV news story from me at the time that raised the question of whether the Mafia had a program to "hire the handicapped" which, when broadcast on television in 1998, sounded a lot less politically incorrect than it does today.

The financial affidavit also stated that Aspirins was a widower with four dependents, whose chief source of income was Social Security disability benefits for himself and additional Social Security payments on behalf of his children. The total income from that source over the past twelve months was about $30,000, according to the affidavit.

But the disabled Aspirins' limited income proved no handicap to his ability to hire defense counsel. Signing on as his lawyer was prominent New York defense attorney Joyce London, who was perhaps best known to the public at that time for representing one of the suspects in the 1993 World Trade Center bombing.

At first, according to the recollection of retired undercover agent Dan DeSimone, it appeared the defendants were set on fighting the charges despite a group plea deal that was being discussed by federal prosecutors. DeSimone remembers a decision was made to put him on the witness stand at early court hearings to put the suspects on notice of what the government had in the way of evidence.

"And at one point it became, 'Dan, we need you to go and testify.'" DeSimone said. "And I walked in the room and raised my right hand, as I recall, and ultimately it was clear amongst them and their attorneys that this guy with the last name of Borelli, who they'd been dealing with for the past several months, wasn't, in fact, somebody named Borelli, but was, in fact, an undercover FBI agent.

"As the story was told to me, shortly after my appearance in court, their attorneys reached back to (FBI Agent) Jerry Hanford and said, 'I think we'd like to take you up on that group plea.'"

Vinnie Aspirins was the first of the outcall case defendants to tumble as part of the group plea deal. In early July 1999, Vinnie "Aspirins" Congiusti pled guilty to conspiracy and aiding and abetting. If he ever got his hands on another drill, it would be in the federal prison tool shed. There was a reason Vinnie Aspirins was first to take the plea deal, according to retired FBI agent Jerry Hanford.

"He was dying, and he wanted to get to a federal medical facility as soon as possible," Hanford said. "He told me that."

Aspirins was sentenced in October of 1999 to forty-one months behind bars. But Vinnie Aspirins would expire well before his sentence would. Less than a year into his prison term, Aspirins died of natural causes on July 29, 2000.

Vinnie Aspirins' drill would end up in the hands of Jerry Hanford, a gift from the FBI on the occasion of his retirement. But Hanford said he isn't sure where the tool is today.

"I'm pretty sure I just got rid of it," Hanford said. "Because the whole thing kinda—it wasn't really something I wanted to have as a memory."

Eventually, as part of the group plea arrangement, all the defendants in the outcall case entered "guilty" pleas to the same conspiracy and aiding and abetting charge that Vinnie Aspirins admitted to.

Mario Pugliese, the reputed Gambino crime family associate, got the most jail time. He was sentenced to sixty-three months in prison. At the court hearing where Pugliese changed his plea to "guilty," he did not admit to any association with organized crime and denied any intent to physically harm anyone. Here's how the *Las Vegas Sun* reported his change of plea, calling Pugliese by his alias of Mario Stefano:

"On Friday, Stefano admitted sending Congiusti and Nelsen to Las Vegas to "bang heads," but said it was just an expression.

"I sent Vinnie Aspirin to confront whoever he could find that was doing wrong, so he could talk to them and, ya know, if he had to, he could threaten them," Stefano said.

He sent Congiusti because he is a "rough-looking guy who could get his point across," Stefano said.

"Vinnie Aspirin, I was told he has a drill, but if he threatens people with it or if he's a legend in his own mind I don't know," Stefano said.

"Stefano also denied that he planned to send two other hired killers to Las Vegas in the days after the arrests."

Kenneth Byrnes was handed a forty-one month sentence in the outcall case. He also pled guilty in Texas to a single criminal count in the money laundering indictment the IRS had been working on since 1996. The government there made a motion for a downward departure in Byrnes' case, requesting the judge impose a lower sentence than recommended by federal guidelines. The government also asked the judge to seal its motion for leniency in Byrnes' case. The federal judge in Texas granted the prosecution's request, sentenced Byrnes to thirty months and allowed him to serve his time in the money laundering case concurrently with his time in the Nevada outcall case. Not a bad deal for Byrnes.

But the best deal, by far, may have been had by Josh Snellings, whose role in the enterprise was mostly as a driver for the other defendants. He was sentenced to credit for time served, which amounted to a little less than a year behind bars.

Anton Nelsen was given a forty-one month sentence for his role in the conspiracy. Contacted by phone for an interview for this book, Nelsen declined, saying, "I'd hate to get my name involved with all this crap again."

Nonetheless, during an eight-minute phone conversation, Nelsen offered a few observations. He conceded that what he got involved with in Las Vegas back in 1998 was "a bad mistake on my part." He also said that today he is a respected member of his community.

As to the FBI investigation, he said, "It was all bullshit." Nelsen said the FBI had, essentially, manufactured the case through its informants.

"They accused me of being with two different Mafia groups," he said. "I'm not even Italian."

Nelsen said he was alleged by authorities to be an explosives expert simply "because I had a can of carburetor fluid." He also said that he did not see where a crime had been committed in his case. He stated that the theft of phone calls was a crime—not trying to put a stop to that theft.

Nelsen also opined, as did Charles Coveney prior to his death, that Coveney's name had been floated as the call diversion mastermind by the FBI. The FBI's case agent in the outcall probe, Charles Maurer, said Kenneth Byrnes, Nelsen's co-conspirator in the outcall case, came up with Coveney's name as a possible call diversion culprit, not the FBI

Chris DeCarlo, whose escort service was at the heart of the investigation, drew a fifty-four month sentence for his role in the case. Attempts to interview DeCarlo for this book were unsuccessful. However, before taking the plea deal, DeCarlo sent the judge a hand-written letter saying he expected to be vindicated at trial and asking the judge to grant him pretrial release from custody.

In the letter, DeCarlo said the government's documents opposing his release were "full of libelous inaccuracies and bold-faced lies."

"The Government would like the Court to believe I am suddenly a danger to the community," DeCarlo wrote. "The Government's opposition inadvertently proves the opposite, in that it states that every alleged act of unrealized violence originated and/or was initiated by Stefano … not DeCarlo."

DeCarlo also denied telling FBI informant Tony Nastasi he was connected to any members of the LCN.

"And I certainly never stated that anyone 'would be given the choice between giving their business over to me or being killed. That statement, in itself, is asinine."

In another part of the letter, DeCarlo denies the allegation he contracted with two Rollin' 60s gang members to get rid of a Philly-linked outcall service owner. DeCarlo admits the two suspects came for a visit from California, but said he had no idea of their "alleged affiliation with a Los Angeles gang and we never discussed killing or harming anyone …

"If it's the Government's assumption that I should have derived that they were gang members simply because they were black, then the Government should be ashamed and reprimanded for such a racist assumption."

Less than three months after writing that letter, DeCarlo would take the same plea deal as the other defendants.

Retired FBI agent Jerry Hanford said he did speak to DeCarlo not long after his arrest in the outcall caper. Hanford said DeCarlo told him the price paid for the services of Vinnie Aspirins and Anton Nelsen was $10,000 each.

"And he said, 'I went to the airport to pick 'em up,'" Hanford recalled. "And he said, 'They're getting off the plane and I see there's the one guy leading the other guy off the plane.' And he said, 'Oh my God, I spent $20,000 for a blind hitman.'"

Whether Vinnie Aspirins was an actual "hitman" (the tabloid "Driller Killer" moniker notwithstanding) was never proven. None of the defendants in the case ever publicly admitted connections to organized crime. Most, if not all, affirmatively denied it.

With plea bargains by all, the FBI outcall investigation concluded, and that marked the end of the official FBI inquiry into the issue of possible corruption inside the Metro Police vice squad and DA's office. None was found. The allegations about phone calls to Las Vegas escort services being intercepted and rerouted were also never confirmed.

"We were never able to uncover any information to verify that the call diversion was going on," said retired agent Charles Maurer. "So, whether it was real, or something they could do temporarily—put it on, take it off—to make it more difficult to detect, we could never verify."

But even though the FBI investigation was over, the allegations of call diversion would not simply go away. One man was about to make getting to the bottom of the call diversion mystery his personal crusade. His unrelenting efforts would take him all the way to the United States Supreme Court, and lead to perhaps the most unusual and controversial hearing in the history of the Nevada Public Utilities Commission. That hearing would feature testimony from a surprise witness who, at the time, was the most notorious computer hacker ever to make the FBI's top ten most wanted list.

Chapter Ten

A Series of Odd Events

"It was a comedy of errors," said Kenneth Byrnes, with a hearty laugh. Byrnes was looking back, more than two decades later, at the odd series of events that landed him in a federal prison where he spent more than three years for his role in the Las Vegas outcall caper. For more than an hour, on the telephone, Byrnes described his involvement in the plan to find whoever was stealing phone calls meant for Chris DeCarlo's escort service and to make the perpetrator stop.

Byrnes is the only surviving member of the outcall conspiracy to agree to an in-depth interview for this book. Byrnes had a lot to say about what happened back in 1998—much of it at odds with what is stated in a criminal complaint and a search warrant affidavit put together by federal authorities who were investigating suspected organized crime involvement in the escort industry.

Byrnes insisted he was never a mobster, soldier, or Mob enforcer. He did, however, concede that Mario Pugliese, aka Mario Stefano, had ties to organized crime. And Mario was clearly calling the shots for Byrnes and the rest of the suspects in the Las Vegas outcall investigation.

Byrnes revealed that Mario's connections were with the Bonanno organized crime family, though, not the Gambinos as the feds initially alleged. Mario and "Johnny Green"

Faraci—an alleged acting capo in the Bonanno family at the time—were connected, said Byrnes. Of course, Mario was also caught telling Tony Nastasi that he had at one time been "with Roy Demeo" who was a known Gambino crime family associate and a particularly violent one at that. Not that Byrnes sees links to a New York crime family—or families—as evidence that what happened in Vegas in 1998 was some sort of Mafia plot.

"Mario may have been hooked up," Byrnes said. "His uncle was a capo in one of the families at one time. He knew a lot of wiseguys, and he hung around with a lot of wiseguys. Listen, if you're from around there (New York/New Jersey), I don't think that's unusual."

Byrnes said it was he, himself, who connected Chris DeCarlo with Mario Pugliese.

"Lucky me. I introduced them," Byrnes offered, somewhat wistfully.

It seems Byrnes had met DeCarlo during the days when Byrnes was running Entertainment Management Services, or EMS, the New Jersey-based credit card processing company that the IRS had accused of laundering money for prostitutes, pimps, and escort services in 1996. Byrnes reported DeCarlo's escort service was one of the agencies that had used EMS to process some credit cards where customers did not want the purchases to appear on their bill as an escort service. Byrnes explained he would run the credit cards through EMS, take out his percentage and funnel the remaining money back to the service owner. Anyone seeing Entertainment Management Services on a credit card bill would more likely think it was for tickets to a show or sporting event than an escort service.

Byrnes said DeCarlo mentioned that he was having problems with his phone system, and Byrnes arranged a meeting with Mario in New York.

"He flew out there to see me and I took him over to see Mario," Byrnes said. "And he discussed, 'Yeah, my phone calls are being stolen and my business is being robbed. I'm losing my clients. They're stealing my calls.'"

A deal was struck with Mario that would eventually lead to the ill-fated trip to Las Vegas by Byrnes, Nelsen, and Vinnie Aspirins to find the source of the call diversion. As former undercover agent Dan DeSimone had suspected, Byrnes confirmed there was a financial agreement between Mario and DeCarlo.

"What the arrangement with Mario was, that if he was able to resolve this situation, and stop this from happening, then DeCarlo would pay Mario—I'm not going to call it 'tribute' because that's absurd—a certain fee at the time, so long as business was profitable."

But the wished-for profits never materialized. Byrnes said he wasn't looking to get rich from outcall anyway, but he'd hoped money would be generated that would help fund the cigarette smuggling operation Mario was also involved in out of the Bahamas. Byrnes revealed he got into the cigarette enterprise after he loaned a hotel owner in the islands $50,000 to help him keep his hotel afloat and pay off debts. It turns out, Byrnes explained, the hotel owner's plan was to buy untaxed cigarettes, smuggle them into the country without tax stamps, sell them for a substantial profit, and use that money to pay off Byrnes and the hotel owner's other debts.

Problem was, the first load of cigarettes was seized by US Customs. Byrnes lost all his money. But, Byrnes said, he could see the scheme itself was solid.

"Clearly, there was smuggling of cigarettes and clearly that was my intention as well. I didn't care at that point, I was chasing that money." Byrnes claimed he also had access to lobster tails that could be imported along with cigarettes for a profit.

What the enterprise needed was someone who had their own boat. Someone like, say, Tony Nastasi.

"We were hoping to get Nastasi to provide a boat," Byrnes said. "The point of the exercise at the time was to impress Nastasi that Mario had more reach, or more influence, than he actually did in order to get Nastasi to play ball and allow him to use that vessel that he claimed he had in Florida."

Nastasi, the FBI informant, had indicated to Mario that he might have access to a vessel, but that was just Nastasi continuing to play his undercover role. There was no boat, although FBI agents probably could have provided one had the undercover operation gone on longer. But the arrest of Mario in New York, and the exposure of Nastasi as an informant, put an end to the smuggling scheme.

"All these disastrous dominos kept falling," Byrnes recalled.

Of Tony Nastasi, Byrnes said, "He was a professional informant. He got paid when he discovered crime. And, you know, his motivations were financial."

Former outcall case agent Charles Maurer said Nastasi was not a paid informant. Mauer said Nastasi was compensated for out-of-pocket expenses, but that probably totaled something in the nature of hundreds of dollars, Maurer said, not thousands or tens of thousands.

It appears Byrnes has little respect for Tony Nastasi. It was, after all, the phone call from Byrnes to Nastasi that led to the FBI raiding DeCarlo's office and arresting everyone. Interestingly, Byrnes asserted that call about Vinnie and his power tools was completely bogus. Byrnes maintained that Mario told him to call Nastasi and invent a story that would make Nastasi think Mario's Vegas crew was making a serious effort to find Coveney and solve Nastasi's problems.

"That was only for his (Nastasi's) benefit. That routine on the phone about Vinnie using the drill."

And it's true Vinnie was not using the drill when FBI agents rushed in. But he did have a drill in his luggage and, as Mario had joked on a wiretapped phone conversation, Vinnie didn't bring the drill with him to put up cabinets.

So, why *was* he packing a Makita?

You can almost see Byrnes shaking his head over the telephone line when he said, "That was him. That was him. (It was) ridiculous."

Byrnes declared Vinnie Aspirins never used a drill on any person as far as he is aware, though he did have that reputation—which The Aspirin probably found useful.

"What Vinnie was doing, I guess, was intimidation by reputation," Byrnes said.

But what about the incident in Tampa, where Vinnie allegedly held a gun to the head of a restaurant owner he was trying to extort? Wasn't that more than mere reputation?

That, Byrnes conceded, actually happened. And Mario had to use his connections with New York's Bonanno crime family to intercede and smooth ruffled feathers, Byrnes disclosed, or it would have been very bad for Vinnie.

"That was just Vinnie being Vinnie," Byrnes suggested. "He tried to shakedown a restaurant owner."

But, despite evidence that Vinnie could put real fear into the heart of a shakedown victim, Byrnes insisted he doesn't accept the notion that Vinnie Aspirins and Anton Nelsen were looking to do him harm once the outcall operation was concluded.

"The prosecutors tried to run that game on me as well," Byrnes said. "They tried to get me to cooperate by suggesting that Vinnie wanted to clip me. And I explained to them: you can take this down the block."

Byrnes indicated that he has never seen a transcript nor heard the recording of Vinnie and Anton talking about going out with Byrnes out for target practice and having an "accidental discharge." He also didn't seem to care much.

"If they did say that, trust me, I knew Vinnie long enough that that was just the usual nonsense and hyperbole." Byrnes said.

Byrnes suggested hyperbole, nonsense, bluster, and bullshit—all recorded on hidden microphones or wiretaps—

comprised the majority of the case against him and the others. For example, Byrnes didn't doubt for a moment that Chris DeCarlo discussed the possibility of whacking outcall service owners with undercover agent Dan DeSimone.

"For him to say it? All day long I could see him doing that," Byrnes said. "Could I see him actually doing something like that? Not a chance."

Of course, that begs the question: If this was all (or mostly) puffery, bluster, and braggadocio, then why did Byrnes ultimately take a deal and enter a guilty plea?

Byrnes claimed he made the decision to plead guilty after his lawyer told him about a letter DeCarlo supposedly wrote to the judge in the case. In the letter, Byrnes divulged, DeCarlo alleges he did the things he did because he was in fear of both the Mob and his own associates who were connected with organized crime. Having an accused co-conspirator state something like that changed the complexion of the case, Byrnes insisted. He decided to join the others in a group plea. Also influencing his decision was the eighteen months he'd already spent awaiting trial in the Clark County Detention Center, certainly an extended-stay facility with beds and breakfast in downtown Las Vegas, but not one you'll find recommended on Yelp.

"Spend enough time in that place and you'll plead guilty to the Lindbergh kidnapping," exclaimed Byrnes.

And while he was setting the record straight from his own perspective, Byrnes took exception to the inference by former undercover agent DeSimone that Byrnes used aluminum baseball bats as tools of his own trade.

"I've always hit with a wooden bat," Byrnes remarked. "But only baseballs (laughs). Not people."

Byrnes asserted that Phil Bunin (now deceased), the man who was being questioned in DeCarlo's office when FBI agents rushed in, was not intimidated or in any way fearful of Vinnie Aspirins and the others. Byrnes expressed he'd known Bunin as a sports betting advisor for years prior to that day and, "Phil was tougher than any of the other guys in that room, trust me."

To this day, Byrnes has no idea if the call diversion allegations that he came to Las Vegas to investigate on behalf of Mario and DeCarlo actually existed.

"I look back now, and I say, was it even real? Or was DeCarlo just making it up? I was getting all my information strictly from DeCarlo (including Coveney's name). I was no computer expert. In fact, I never sent an email until long after I got out of prison."

Which begs another question: If neither Byrnes nor the other conspirators were computer experts, what made them think they could resolve a phone hacking scheme in favor of DeCarlo? And for that matter, if they felt the call stealing was real, and a crime, why didn't they encourage DeCarlo go to the police or the FBI rather than seeking help from Mario Pugliese (aka Stefano)?

"And you know what? You're right," acknowledged Byrnes. "Of course, that wasn't my mindset at the time. It just didn't occur to me that that's what he should do."

Byrnes said DeCarlo gave him the impression of being a wiseguy wannabe, a young man more enamored with the prospect of becoming connected with organized crime than he was of resolving the phone call diversion mystery.

"It wasn't just satisfactory to get this straightened out. He always wanted to take it to another level," Byrnes opined.

"Another level" of intrigue might well describe DeCarlo's involvement with the Rollin' 60s gangsters from L.A., allegedly brought into Las Vegas to get rid of a Philly-linked outcall service owner.

"I do remember that wacko bullshit," said Byrnes. "In fact, that's where the damn guns came from, DeCarlo bringing in these Rollin' 60s. What the hell is a Rollin' 60? That's where those weapons came from."

In the intervening decades since Byrnes was released from prison, he has not re-offended. He contends that anything he did back in Vegas in 1998 was far less serious than the hacking of the phone system and the theft of phone calls—if that was really going on. It's something he thinks law enforcement should have gotten to the bottom of.

"And that is one issue that was never, ever seemingly explored by the FBI or the District Attorney at the time. They didn't seem to have the least bit of interest, actually, in looking into that at all."

Asked what he is doing today—Byrnes wanted to be vague. Like Anton Nelsen, he's currently a well-respected member of his community and he works with people who are unaware of his past involvement with the FBI's outcall probe.

"If you want to tell people Ken Byrnes is living comfortably in Edmonton (Alberta, Canada), that would be just fine," Byrnes joked.

Chapter Eleven

Aftermath

On Monday, January 4, 1999, many Las Vegans retrieved their evening *Las Vegas Sun* newspaper from front porches and driveways hoping, perhaps, to read in the sports section about the previous day's NFL playoffs. In addition to the expected football coverage on the sports page, readers also found this odd item in the local news section:

Sprint Robbers Get High-Tech Equipment They Wanted

By Jace Radke

Robbers in ski masks who rushed employees at a Sprint telephone company central office stole exactly what they were looking for—high-tech computerized phone equipment—officials said today.

'It appears that they took what they went in there for,' Metro Police Spokesman Steve Meriwether said regarding the 8 a.m. Sunday theft at the Sprint office on Spring Mountain Road just north of Jones Boulevard.

The robbery, in which a man and women employees were attacked with stun guns and a male phone company contractor was stunned and beaten, left about 75,000 customers in southwest Las Vegas without phone service for much of Sunday morning, Sprint officials said.

'About ninety percent of service was restored by 1:30 p.m. and the rest by about 2:30 p.m.,' Sprint spokeswoman Detra Page said. 'This is very unusual. We're never had anything like this happen before.'

Indeed, no one could remember a crime remotely similar to this. Even by Vegas standards, it was a uniquely bizarre heist. Who would risk a long stretch in a penitentiary to rob a telephone office and hijack computerized call switching equipment? It wasn't like you could haul these highly specialized electronic devices down to the local pawn shop like a cell phone or laptop and hock them for quick cash. And, even if you could find a fence for a load of hot hardware, who would buy stolen, call-switching equipment? A pirate phone company?

It was an outlandish crime that mystified practically the entire city of Las Vegas. But not everyone.

There was one man in particular who thought he knew who was behind this violent and curious crime. That man was Eddie Munoz, outcall entertainment service owner and adult entertainment promoter. The robbery at the Sprint telephone switching center happened a few months after the FBI's investigation into call diversion in the escort industry was made public and Munoz immediately suspected there was a connection between the unusual equipment theft and the alleged theft of phone calls meant for outcall entertainment services.

While watching news coverage of the aftermath of the Sprint robbery on local television, one of Munoz's employees said she recognized a Sprint telephone worker she had seen going in and out of the building with police.

Munoz's employee had previously worked as a phone girl for one of the top escort services in Las Vegas. She told

Munoz that the Sprint worker she recognized in the news footage of the robbery was a regular visitor to the escort service where she used to work. She clarified that the man was not a customer, but an apparent friend or business associate of the owner. This Intel about the telephone worker was one more piece of the puzzle for Munoz. He believed the only people bold enough to risk prison to rip off telephone switching computers would be people who knew how to put them to use for a substantial profit: phone hackers, especially if those hackers had links to the escort industry.

As it turns out, federal authorities eventually arrested and indicted five men in the robbery, though it was 2002 before the whole gang was rounded up. The motive for the robbery, according to federal agents, was much more mundane than intercepting phone calls. The reason for the heist, FBI agents said, was to steal computer circuit boards that could be resold for a substantial profit. Agents estimated the value of the circuit boards at $1.5 million. Some members of the gang had previously sold similar computer parts to various companies that specialized in refurbishing and reselling telecommunications equipment.

Munoz wasn't so sure he accepted the FBI's explanation, but even if it was true, he felt the robbery substantiated a concern he'd held for years: that the telephone infrastructure, especially in Las Vegas, was vulnerable to attack, both physically and electronically.

Munoz had been reporting strange problems with his business phone lines since at least 1991, though initially it was not the diversion of calls. Originally, Munoz said, calls to his outcall entertainment service seemed like they were being monitored. When he sent a woman to meet a client in a hotel room, often another woman from a different service would show up to the same call minutes ahead of his employee who, upon arrival, would find the other escort already in the process of "entertaining" the client.

At first, Munoz thought some clients had merely called two different services and his rivals had simply gotten there first. But, like Helga, the outcall madam mentioned in Chapter Two of this book, Munoz started checking with the clients when these "double dates" happened and discovered several incidents where phone records on the client's hotel bill showed solely the call to Munoz's service.

"They'd have a girl beat us to a call, and they knew exactly what had been told by the guy to our girl over the phone," Munoz asserted.

Though a customer could have called Munoz's service on his room phone and another outcall agency with a cell phone, it didn't seem likely to be a repeated scenario. The calls would have to have been made in close proximity to each other for the women to arrive at the hotel room almost simultaneously, and what would be the advantage of using two different phone systems to book dates with two different services?

About the time he started experiencing phone problems, Munoz explained he was told about a method that could boost his business. For a modest fee upfront, and a percentage of the profits later, there was a group that could intercept phone calls meant for other outcall services and divert those calls to Munoz's service.

"People started approaching me—we want to offer you this for so much a call," Munoz continued. "I thought I was being set up, so I said no."

After his refusal to get involved in a call diversion scheme, Munoz asserted his phone problems got even worse.

"Then they put me on the dark side, and my phones didn't ring at all."

The person who had initially approached him with information about a group which was able to divert phone calls, Munoz said, was a six foot, two inches tall former phone phreak, rock groupie, prostitute, and computer hacker named Susan Headley, also known as Susy Thunder.

Thunder was one of several young hackers profiled in the 1991 book *Cyberpunk*.

Police records show Susy Thunder had a work card in Las Vegas to deal table games at the Four Queens Casino from 1997-1999. She was also registered as a proposition poker player at the Stardust from 1996-1999.

These dates cover the time when allegations of call diversion were being investigated by the FBI in Las Vegas as part of its overall outcall probe. Her Las Vegas Metro police work card photograph is included in this book.

Although there's no Metro police record of her having a work card as an escort or outcall entertainer, Munoz said he employed Susy Thunder for a time along the Arizona-Nevada border.

At that time, Munoz said, adult entertainers often performed without getting work cards because the outcall services were in the midst of a fight with county regulators over the work card requirement.

"She was working for my service in Laughlin. She had a great personality. She would actually get compliments. Big girl, big hips."

Munoz showed me adult publications, dating back to December of 1992, displaying pictures of Thunder, provocatively clad, in Southern Nevada personal ads using stage names like "Sexy Serena" and "Janine." In the "Janine" ad, the text mentions Thunder's unusual size.

"Let me show you every delicious inch of my six-foot-tall body," the ad read. A copy of that ad can be found in this book. The name she uses, "Janine," is also a name she went by during her call girl days in Southern California, according to the book *Cyberpunk*.

Susy Thunder made no bones about having been both a hooker and a hacker. In a story published in *Esquire* magazine in 1995, *Cyberpunk* co-author Katie Hafner chronicles a trip with Susy to Las Vegas at a time when Hafner was trying to arrange a meeting with the then-notorious computer hacker

Kevin Mitnick, who was a friend of Susy's and who would become the 1990s poster boy for electronic intrusion. A portion of the article describes the Las Vegas jaunt:

> *At six two, Susan towers over most other women. With long, straight blond hair, a full figure, and a big overbite, she is Joni Mitchell writ large. Her background is similarly expansive: An eighth-grade dropout turned Hollywood streetwalker, she fell in with phone phreaks, turned her attention to breaking into computers, then, incredibly enough, in 1994 was elected city clerk in a small California desert town.*
>
> *Susan and I check into the Gold Coast, a no-frills hotel and casino on the south side of town favored by the locals. She stretches all seventy-four inches across the bed and begins leafing through the "Entertainers" section of the Yellow Pages in search of Ginger, a former colleague. She lingers over the photographs of women in various seductive poses. She claims to know a few of them and offers comments, as if looking through her old high school yearbook. She's hoping Ginger can send a few tricks her way, so she can make enough money to go visit Kevin in prison."*

Munoz believes Ginger, the woman Thunder mentions in the *Esquire* article, was Munoz's own, late wife Virginia, who Munoz said was a friend of Susy's. Virginia, according to Munoz, at one time dated Eddie Escobedo, the *El Mundo* publisher and close friend of Charles Coveney. That's a kind of Kevin Bacon-esque, two-degrees of separation between Coveney and Thunder, but it's interesting to note that Coveney and Thunder not only shared an interest and expertise in computers, but both were also semi-professional poker players in Las Vegas during the same time period. Is it possible they met and had much in common to talk about?

Not according to Coveney. During our one-and-only interview prior to his death, Coveney said he did not recognize the name Headley or Thunder when I asked him about her. Thunder also never surfaced as even a blip on the FBI's radar during the Bureau's Las Vegas outcall investigation. This, despite the fact that her personal experience in the escort industry, her knowledge of computer hacking, and her past record of manipulating the telephone system would seem to make Thunder an obvious person of interest, especially since she held work cards for various occupations in Las Vegas during the period of time when the call diversion allegations were being investigated. But retired FBI agent Charles Maurer said Thunder's name was never heard on any wiretaps, and agents never received any information about her during their outcall probe. She was never investigated or charged with anything involving the Las Vegas call diversion allegations.

Interestingly, as written in *Cyberpunk*, during the early 1990s, when Thunder and Mitnick were both living and working in Las Vegas, Thunder claimed to have employed Mitnick as what she vaguely refers to as a "telecommunications specialist."

That speaks nothing about call diversion. But given Thunder's escort industry experience, her phone phreaking, and Mitnick's own expertise in computers and phone hacking—the term "telecommunications specialist" certainly sounds intriguing.

Mitnick was able to flee justice in a cross-country spree between 1992 and his eventual arrest in 1995, after being indicted for computer crimes. Those crimes did not involve the Las Vegas telephone system, though Mitnick would later admit he hacked the Las Vegas Sprint system while a fugitive in order to thwart federal agents who were trying to track his communications.

Mitnick, through his publicist, declined an interview for this book, citing circumstances that were only described as "conflicting but not competing." A woman answering a phone linked to Thunder claimed to be her sister and said she would forward a request for comment to Susy. No response was received.

Eddie Munoz would eventually enlist Kevin Mitnick's aid in trying to prove the call diversion allegations were true. But not until after Mitnick was released from prison in January 2000.

When news broke of the arrests of Vinnie Aspirins and crew in 1998, Munoz hoped the full story of the phone call diversion situation would soon be given a public airing. But the plea bargains taken by all of the defendants marked the end of the FBI outcall probe, and also put an end to the prospect of a trial. That meant the vast majority of evidence collected by federal agents would never surface in court and would remain unseen and unheard by the public.

It was a bitter disappointment for Munoz.

But Munoz wasn't about to let the issue slide, and he would spend a great deal of his own time and money in an effort to prove phone calls had been diverted and to bring those responsible for the hacking to account.

Munoz fought his war on two fronts. The first was the Nevada Public Utilities Commission (PUC), the regulatory agency that had oversight of the telephone network in the state. If he lost there, he would appeal any adverse decision to the courts, and wage a legal battle.

For years, Munoz had been collecting information and evidence about the suspected phone call diversion and/or call monitoring. But his evidence was largely circumstantial, consisting mostly of hundreds of pages of call logs from his business and "trouble tickets" generated by the phone company when he complained about his problems.

For his PUC hearing, however, Munoz hired a lawyer, a private investigator, and an eyebrow-raising technical expert.

He also brought to the witness stand additional alleged victims of call diversion or unauthorized call monitoring in Las Vegas. Those witnesses included other adult business owners, a private eye, and a bail bondsman.

In March 2002, more than three years after the FBI took down Vinnie Aspirins and crew, hearings finally got underway in Las Vegas before the PUC in Docket No. 00-6057, the case of *Eddie Munoz vs. Sprint Telephone of Nevada*. Munoz asserted that Sprint was at fault for a loss of business at Munoz's outcall entertainment service by failing to secure its phone lines. Munoz would ultimately seek $30 million from Sprint for lost, dropped, or diverted telephone calls.

Among the first of Munoz's witnesses to testify was Larry Reubel, a dapper, sixty-something former businessman who had retired to a small town in Utah after his Las Vegas adult entertainment company had gone belly-up. Reubel published the pamphlets handed out by some outcall service owners promoting their "entertainers." Reubel got a piece of each transaction between the entertainers and their customers.

That is, until business suddenly and dramatically dropped off. The precipitous decline in revenue, according to Reubel, was likely due to theft of phone calls by hackers.

Former-phone-hacker-turned-tech-journalist Kevin Poulsen covered the hearing for the online publication *Security Focus*. Here's how he described Reubel's cross examination by Patrick Riley, one of the outside lawyers hired by Sprint:

> *Going over your testimony, you seem to blame Sprint for the loss of your business, Riley said, with mock bewilderment. Is that correct?*

> *They're providing a service to me, and they're not providing the security they should," Reubel replied. So, yes.*

Riley countered by carefully outlining all the steps the phone company took to investigate Reubel's complaint when he first raised it in 1995: Sprint made test calls to Reubel's numbers, and they all went through. They ran a script at their switching control center that periodically checked his lines for covert call forwarding, never finding any. They examined his lines for physical taps, and there were none.

"Doesn't it look like Sprint went to an awful lot of trouble to investigate your complaint?" Riley asked reasonably.

Reubel smiled without humor, leaned into the microphone and spoke slowly. "I was making a quarter million dollars a year. I'm making ten dollars an hour now. Whatever they did, it wasn't enough."

And there were other witnesses whose businesses also relied on telephone traffic who told the same tale: their phones had suddenly stopped ringing, despite increased spending on advertising and despite the fact that their services were in demand in Las Vegas which, at the time, was the fastest growing metropolitan area in the country. A rising tide of commerce should have been lifting all boats, but these people all found themselves in the same boat and that boat was foundering.

As sad and heartfelt as their stories were, it was anecdotal evidence. It was not proof.

But, the most compelling witness for Munoz was still to come, although he almost didn't make it to the witness stand. A dispute over payment nearly kept reformed computer hacker Kevin Mitnick from testifying but, at the last minute, he and Munoz worked out an arrangement.

When Mitnick did start speaking, under oath, his testimony was electric. Mitnick was, at that time, probably the most notorious former hacker in the nation's history. After his arrest in 1995, Mitnick spent five years in prison before being released and eventually becoming a cyber security consultant.

It wasn't just his skill at entering and perusing, with ease, government and private computers that made Mitnick a cult figure among computer nerds and tech-heads. Like a cybernetic cat burglar, he was also able to stay one step ahead of the FBI during his time as a fugitive. That element of being an outlaw on a new frontier also contributed to his status as a legend in the hacker community.

One of the ways Mitnick was able to keep from being captured during two years on the run was to hack into various telephone systems to keep his phone calls from being traced by federal agents. One of the systems he compromised during his time as a fugitive, he said, was the Las Vegas telephone network which was run by Sprint. His PUC testimony flew directly in the face of earlier testimony by Sprint security officials who maintained that the company's lines were secure and, as far as they were concerned, had never been compromised. Mitnick testified that he hacked the Las Vegas phone network through a system used by Sprint known as Centralized Automated Loop Reporting System (CALRS), pronounced "callers."

Reported Kevin Poulsen in *Security Focus*:

> *Mitnick's claims seemed to inspire skepticism in the PUC's technical advisor, who asked the ex-hacker, shortly before the hearing was to break for lunch, if he could prove that he had cracked Sprint's network. Mitnick said he would try.*

> *Two hours later, Mitnick returned to the hearing room clutching a crumpled, dog-eared, and torn sheet of paper, and a small stack of copies for the commissioner, lawyers, and staff.*

> *At the top of the paper was printed "3703-03 Remote Access Password List." A column listed 100 "seeds," numbered "00" through "99," corresponding to a column of four-digit hexadecimal "passwords," like d4d5 and 1554.*

Commissioner Escobar Chanos accepted the list as an exhibit over the objections of Sprint attorney Patrick Riley, who complained that it hadn't been provided to the company in discovery. Mitnick retook the stand and explained that he used the lunch break to visit a nearby storage locker that he'd rented on a long-term basis, years ago, before his arrest. "I wasn't sure if I had it in that storage locker," said Mitnick. "I hadn't been there in seven years."

"If the system is still in place, and they haven't changed the seed list, you could use this to get access to CALRS," Mitnick testified. "The system would allow you to wiretap a line or seize dial tone."

Kevin Poulsen, himself a former phone phreak, found Mitnick's testimony powerful and persuasive.

"He definitely knew exactly what he was talking about," Poulsen told me in an interview for this book. "He didn't over-reach. He didn't claim that he had evidence that Munoz was a victim. But he talked about how much access he had when he was a hacker and from what period of time, and how he did it. So, clearly, he established—and they did nothing to effectively shoot this down—clearly established that they had the same security holes that pretty much every phone company had in the 80s and 90s. Except, unlike other phone companies, they just didn't know it. And they did nothing to stop it."

But would it have been possible for someone to hijack the phone system and reroute calls meant for one escort service to another?

Poulsen said he was personally involved in hacking the phone system in Los Angeles in the early 1990s in connection with an escort service operation. Poulsen had a friend in the escort trade, and that friend showed Poulsen Yellow Page ads for escort services that had gone out of business.

Poulsen, using his phone-hacking skills, was able to reconnect the disconnected phone numbers that were listed in the phone book ads and direct calls meant for those numbers to his friend's escort service. That gave his friend free telephone lines and free Yellow Page ads (worth as much as $3,000 a month per ad). The friend then shared part of the profits from his escort business with Poulsen. Poulsen later found out that many of the numbers he re-connected had originally been shut down by court orders as a result of L.A. police vice investigations. When the vice cops found out the numbers they had worked so hard to disconnect had been reconnected, they eventually tracked Poulsen down and arrested him.

Poulsen suggested the same techniques he used to reactivate dormant Yellow Page numbers could have been used by hackers in Vegas to divert calls from one escort service to another.

"It's totally plausible," Poulsen admitted. "I could have done it back in the day. It would have been just as easy to temporarily divert calls from existing numbers as it was to reconnect disconnected ones."

Poulsen conceded his method would be detectable if someone knew where to look, but he seriously doubted Sprint had the necessary security protocols in place at that time to uncover such a call diversion scheme.

"It would leave a trace, but not one that they would have picked up on."

The regulatory staff of the Nevada Public Utilities Commission seemed to agree with Poulsen about the state of security in the Las Vegas phone system in the mid-to-late 1990s.

In its post-hearing brief regarding the Munoz case, PUC staff had sharp words for Sprint and the utility's past record on the detection or prevention of hacking.

Staff members wrote:

Although vast technological changes have occurred since 1995, Sprint witness' testimony in this record about its own security practices provides this commission with little or no assurance that the Nevada Sprint telephone system is secure. Mr. Munoz, Mr. Mitnick, and public witness Stewart Nelkin also believe that Sprint's security practices jeopardize national security.

The record demonstrates how little Nevada Sprint is telling, even in general terms, about its most basic security practices and procedures. Evidence in the record from Sprint's own witness establishes that Sprint's switch log and data retention policies have prevented Sprint from systematically analyzing intrusion attempts and system vulnerabilities. While staff concludes that numerous factors may be contributing to Mr. Munoz service problems, this complaint has revealed significant Sprint specific security issues that require prompt and thorough regulatory review.

While articulating serious concerns about the state of security in the Las Vegas phone system, the PUC staff recommended that the Munoz complaint be dismissed, essentially because the record had established that while hacking *could* be the cause of Munoz's phone problems, he had not demonstrated it *was* the cause of the problems. But the staff also indicated the security issues identified in the hearings were such that the commission should order Sprint to hire consultants and work with the Commission staff to resolve those issues.

But the politically appointed Commission did not adopt all of the recommendations from its staff. It did elect to dismiss Munoz's complaint. But the Commission clearly did not share the staff's concern that there were security issues within Sprint that required prompt, additional review. In its order to dismiss the Munoz complaint, the commission also dismissed the staff recommendation that Sprint be directed to hire security consultants, saying:

> *As to the first issue of call diversion and/or call blockage, the record does not present evidence that Sprint has caused either to occur...*

> *As to the second issue, the record does not present sufficient evidence that Sprint has failed to take the necessary precautions to insure the security of its network...*

> *The record further supports that Sprint's network security is no better nor no (sic) worse than that of other telephone companies.*

> *The commission does not find substantial evidence on the record to support the complaint that Sprint has not taken reasonable steps to protect the security of its network. Therefore, the Commission finds that it should dismiss the complaint.*

And, with that, Eddie Munoz struck out with the Nevada Public Utilities Commission.

As to whether Munoz's problems may have been caused by people hacking into Sprint or by corrupt technicians gaffing local hotel switchboards—as Charles Coveney suggested shortly before his death—Kevin Poulsen declared the better of the two methods, from a hacker's perspective, would be a breach of Sprint.

The reason: a phone company hack would give the hacker control of all calls in the area, not just those from a selected number of hotels. In fact, Poulsen offered, it might have been even easier to hack Sprint than to plant a device in multiple hotel switchboards.

"You only have to get access in one place if you hack the phone company. Doesn't matter where the person is calling from, doesn't matter what hotel they're in," Poulsen explained. "You still get the call rather than having to get into a dozen different hotels."

Munoz remained convinced the fault lay with Sprint. But he was running out of money and was acting as his own attorney when he took his case to the United States District Court of Nevada. He would have no luck there, either. Munoz claimed he was misled about how much time he had to file an appeal of his PUC case. As it turned out, he didn't get his case before the court during the time window provided to appeal a state regulatory decision. The court tossed the case because it wasn't filed in a timely manner.

Munoz appealed the decision to the Ninth Circuit Court of Appeals and lost there. Now, his only recourse was the highest court in the land: The United States Supreme Court. The High Court refused to hear his case. From a legal standpoint, his fight to prove he was the victim of call diversion was over.

For the Las Vegas FBI, the issue of call diversion was something agents had hoped to unravel in their investigation of alleged Mob influence in the escort industry. But Vinnie Aspirins and his drill had forced investigators to close the case early and arrest the Mob-linked conspirators before anyone got hurt, especially the targeted outcall service owners.

"I'm absolutely certain that we prevented physical harm from coming to Bartello and Soranno," retired federal agent Maurer asserted.

But as for the call stealing allegations? Neither the alleged enforcers sent by Mario Pugliese nor the FBI itself was really in a position to get to the bottom of that aspect of the case back in 1998.

Said retired Federal Agent Jerry Hanford, "The problem the FBI had when all the computer crimes started, they wouldn't admit that they didn't have the capability to do it (solve the crimes). So, they took their own people and tried to train them to be computer experts. Good people—working hard—but they didn't have the expertise they really needed."

In a sense, the allegations of phone call diversion, or the notion that someone had a "black box" that could redirect phone calls from one escort service to another, is much like the proverbial "MacGuffin" in suspense movies. It's the object that everyone in the movie is chasing, whether it be uranium, smuggled diamonds, or plans for a secret weapon. The nature of the object itself is secondary to its role in advancing the story.

In the Las Vegas outcall investigation, the MacGuffin would have been the call stealing "black box" or perhaps even computer expert Charles Coveney, the thing the suspects were chasing while the federal agents chased them.

Whether this MacGuffin—a call diversion device or a computer expert hacking the phone system—was real or imagined may forever remain an unsolved mystery.

"The only way it would be solved would be if a culprit actually stepped forward and admitted to it," said Kevin Poulsen. "And provided enough detail to make it convincing."

Genuine or not, investigators say, the call diversion allegations were real enough to the people pursuing Charles Coveney to put lives in danger.

"Chris DeCarlo believed it," retired agent Maurer notes, wryly, "And believed it enough to set in motion a plan to kill two people."

What Happened to …?

In the intervening decades since the 1998 FBI probe into organized crime influence in the escort industry in Las Vegas, little has changed in the way business in that industry is conducted. Outcall entertainers are still called to the hotel rooms of guests seeking an experience with sex workers. Police officials still say the majority of these "entertainers" are prostitutes looking to connect with clients.

But internet technology has had a significant impact on how customers and purveyors of sex services hook up. A *Las Vegas Sun* newspaper article from the late 1990s notes that there were more than 150 outcall entertainment services licensed in Clark County, Nevada, at that time. At the time of the publication of this book, that number had dwindled to less than forty, despite the Las Vegas metro area being one of the fastest growing population centers in the US.

One reason for the lower number of outcall services, some sex industry researchers believe, is that sex workers found a way, via the internet, to reach customers directly through websites like Backpage.com, Redbook, the personals sections of Craigslist, and specific cell phone apps which have facilitated the ease with which this can be accomplished. Phone books have been displaced by Facebooks. The physical Yellow Pages, once a significant source of outcall advertising, are virtually non-existent today. Adult services are now largely advertised over the internet. And the internet also provides a direct connection between the buyer and the seller. No need, with the right kind of website or app, to employ a pimp, madam, or agency as a middleman. And with no middleman, the sex worker can also pocket the middleman's profit.

"I think the internet significantly changed the industry," said former ACLU lawyer Allen Lichtenstein. "You don't need to have the larger companies and you don't need to have the news racks or handbillers. Not that they aren't still out there—but there are not that many of them."

Lichtenstein said it's ironic, but technology, which made advertising, locating, and promoting sex work more user-friendly, seems to have also done more to lessen the impact and visibility of escort services than police stings or county laws attempting to regulate their advertising.

"Often times the authorities are trying to get rid of something and can't do it legally—but it ends up fading away based on new technology and different marketing based on that new technology."

However, the FBI has shut down Backpage.com and is targeting other, similar sites, as part of an intense, ongoing effort to combat human-trafficking and the exploitation of children in the sex trade. This could dramatically change the dynamic for adult sex workers once again.

"The internet and sites like *Backpage* allowed (adult) individuals to, in essence, run their own business," said UNLV sex industry researcher, and professor, Barbara Brents. "They could screen their own clients—they didn't need a third-party manager."

"What we're seeing now is the decline of the middle-class call girl," said Brents. "What's left is either the more desperate people that are having to go to the streets, or super high-end people who have their own websites with multiple computers and whatever else they use to do things."

Brents said the demise of Backpage.com, and possibly other sites in the near future, means sex workers with limited resources will have to find new ways to connect with the right kind of clients who won't do them any harm.

"Now, the more you're making it harder for people to do this work—screening and keeping themselves safe on their own—it's leaving it ripe for third party managers to come in and take over."

Most knowledgeable observers of the Las Vegas sex trade believe the outcall entertainment business model probably peaked in the 1990s, and the escort agencies may never again be as numerous or as profitable. Even if they get a benefit from the demise of websites targeted by law enforcement for human trafficking violations, the advertising for the outcall services will undoubtedly be primarily online or in cyberspace, and not so much on the streets or in news racks. That will certainly keep the industry's public profile lower than it was in the 1990s.

Only time will tell if a period of revitalization is in store for outcall or escort services in Las Vegas. Perhaps an entirely new technology will come along to alter the way sex workers connect with clients.

"No matter what emerges," said Lichtenstein, "It will lessen neither the demand nor the supply (for sex work)."

As for what has happened, in the intervening decades, to the people connected to the 1998 outcall industry investigation profiled in this book, there is less need for speculation because more definitive information is available. A few people connected to the 1998 case have died, others have retired, and some are still working.

Here is a list of those people with their current status, to the extent the authors have been able to determine, at the time of publication:

CHARLES COVENEY. As mentioned elsewhere in this book, Charles Coveney died in 2012 from lingering complications due to diabetes and heart surgery. Whatever secrets, if any, he held about phone call diversion in connection with Las Vegas escort services, he took with him to his grave.

RICHARD SORANNO. Considered the top outcall service owner at the time of the FBI's 1998 investigation, Richard Soranno died May 18, 2009, in Las Vegas. He was fifty-three. His obituary in a newspaper in his home state of New Jersey said he died suddenly, after a short illness. According to the Clark County Coroner's office, his manner of death was suicide, his cause of death a self-inflicted gunshot wound to the torso.

CHRISTIANO DECARLO. DeCarlo, like others who pled guilty in the Las Vegas outcall investigation, did his time and was released from prison. However, following his release, this former outcall service owner got involved in a domestic situation in 2009 that led to a stand-off with Las Vegas Metro Police. During the course of that incident, DeCarlo shot himself in the chest, but survived. He did additional time for being an ex-felon in possession of a firearm, but eventually got out of prison on that charge as well. At one time his federal supervision, which followed his release from prison, was transferred from Las Vegas to North Dakota, but social media accounts suggest DeCarlo may have moved back to Las Vegas after that. As mentioned earlier, attempts to obtain a comment from him for this book were unsuccessful.

VINNIE "ASPIRINS" CONGIUSTI. As mentioned earlier in this book, Vinnie "Aspirins" died in a federal prison while serving his sentence for crimes connected to the outcall probe. He was the ripe old age of fifty at the time of his death.

ANTON NELSEN. Anton Nelsen did his prison time in connection with the outcall case and was released on September 28, 2001. If Nelsen, as Mario Pugliese once suggested, had blown up his own dentist's office (never proved), then his post-prison career took him in the opposite direction. He was last reported operating a construction company in southeast Texas, where he is known as a builder. He has no history of any additional federal offenses.

JOSH SNELLINGS. The alleged driver for the outcall conspirators, Snellings, as reported earlier in this book, was released from jail with credit for time served. There's no evidence he was ever involved in other federal crimes.

KENNETH BYRNES. As mentioned earlier, Byrnes pleaded guilty in both the Las Vegas outcall case and the IRS money laundering case out of Dallas, Texas, involving payments to pimps and prostitutes. He did his time in both cases concurrently and was released the same day as Anton Nelsen, September 28, 2001. There's no evidence of Byrnes being involved in any additional federal crimes. He's believed to be self-employed and would like you to believe he's living somewhere in Alaska. A remote part of Alaska.

MARIO PUGLIESE, aka MARIO STEFANO. The alleged Gambino and/or Bonanno crime family associate did his time and was released from prison March 8, 2004. He died March 16, 2012, apparently of natural causes. At the time of his death, Stefano was being sued civilly for alleged fraud by the transportation company CSX, which accused Stefano of booking services from CSX that were never paid for.

DANIEL DESIMONE. DeSimone, the FBI agent who acted in an undercover capacity as Tony Nastasi's outcall service manager, "Danny Borelli," went on to become a chief of FBI undercover operations. He retired from the FBI in 2011. He reminds Americans that danger and sacrifice are a daily part of life for undercover agents in all areas of law enforcement, and points to the importance of their role in keeping the country safe.

TONY NASTASI. The former outcall service owner who became an FBI informant received a bit of notoriety on (ironically) Valentine's Day 2001 when he testified in the case of rapper Sean "Puffy" Combs. Combs had been accused of throwing a gun out of a vehicle following a shooting at a New York nightclub and a limousine driver Nastasi employed witnessed the incident and found the gun. In 2002, Nastasi was arrested in connection with a call girl investigation by the NYPD involving Nastasi's business, Casablanca Escorts. Nastasi eventually pleaded guilty to attempted money laundering, second degree, in that case and was sentenced to thirty days in jail with five years' probation to follow. That was in 2003. He was last reported to be living somewhere on Long Island, New York.

CHARLES MAURER. Charles "Charlie" Maurer, the case agent for the FBI's 1998 outcall investigation, retired from the FBI in 2002 and went to work for a time as a supervisor for the Federal Air Marshal Service. He is now completely retired from federal service.

JERRY HANFORD. Jerry Hanford retired from the FBI in 2003 and left Las Vegas. Although he disposed of Vinnie Aspirins' drill after receiving it as a tongue-in-cheek retirement gift, Hanford does continue to possess the switchblade knife Aspirins was carrying when he was arrested.

KEN "KENJI" GALLO. This former hoodlum and associate of the Los Angeles Mafia, who reformed and became an informant for the FBI, now operates an upscale, mixed martial arts gym in the upper Midwest. He wrote his own book about his experiences in organized crime called, *Breakshot: A Life in the 21st Century American Mafia.*

KEVIN MITNICK. This one-time FBI "most wanted" computer hacker has become a cyber security consultant after serving time in a federal penitentiary. His business is located in Henderson, Nevada, which is adjacent to Las Vegas. Outcall service owner Eddie Munoz was one of Mitnick's early consulting clients.

SUSY THUNDER. This former prostitute, phone phreak, and computer hacker was never a target or subject of the Las Vegas outcall investigation, although outcall service owner Eddie Munoz alleges she offered to put him in touch with people who knew how to divert phone calls from one escort service to another. As reported earlier in this book, attempts to obtain a comment from her were unsuccessful. Sources indicate she now lives a quiet life in the largest city of a populous Midwestern state.

EDDIE MUNOZ. This adult entertainment business owner, who fought for years to have his claims of hacking and telephone call diversion taken seriously, still grinds out a living in the adult entertainment industry in Las Vegas. He also publishes G-rated brochures directing visitors to various museums and other attractions in the Las Vegas area. Munoz maintains to this day that phone calls to his business were intercepted and diverted, and he continues to sound the alarm about the dangers of telephone and computer hacking.

THE END

ACKNOWLEDGEMENTS

The story you have just read has been begging to be told for more than two decades. Many people helped to bring this crime caper to the public eye, and the authors want to express our sincere gratitude to those who don't mind being recognized.

First and foremost, we thank retired FBI Special Agent Charles Maurer, who served as the case agent for the investigation at the heart of this book. He spent hours unselfishly sharing his memories and recollections with the authors regarding the events and personalities involved. His co-case agent Jerry Hanford also deserves thanks for the insights he provided into the case.

We'd also like to thank Jack Sheehan, author of his own book about the Las Vegas skin trade and a long-time observer of organized crime's influence in Las Vegas. Gratitude goes to Eddie Munoz for his insight into the business of outcall entertainment, and UNLV professors Barbara Brents and Candice Michelle Seppa Arroyo, for sharing their observations and knowledge of the Las Vegas sex industry from an academic perspective, while UNLV's Michael Green provided a historical perspective. Our appreciation also goes out to former UNLV professor and documentary filmmaker Stan Armstrong for his support.

Thanks also to Mike Bindrup, David Raymond, and William Coveney for their memories of Charles Coveney, one of the key players in this tale. Special thanks to Ken

"Kenji" Gallo who not only played an active, undercover role in the 1998 FBI investigation of escort services but provided the authors with anecdotes and revelations never before made public about the case.

Shoutouts also go to cooperating witness Tony Nastasi and retired FBI agent Daniel DeSimone, aka "Danny Borelli," who were the "inside" guys in the FBI escort service probe.

Additionally, we want to acknowledge some of the journalists for the print and electronic media who reported early on about elements of this case: George Knapp, Daniel Green, Peter O'Connell, John L. Smith, Kim Smith, Karen Zekan, Bill Gang, Jace Radke, Katie Hafner and, particularly, Kevin Poulsen, himself a former hacker and phone phreak who offered us his own observations and experience regarding the possible interception and diversion of phone calls meant for escort services.

Thanks to Louise Uttinger, counsel for the Nevada Public Utilities Commission. Though she declined an interview for this book, she pointed the way to public records that helped flesh out the regulatory investigation into allegations of call diversion in the escort industry.

Finally, special thanks go out anonymously to several folks who would rather not have their names included in the book at this point. We know you have your reasons. But we want to acknowledge your contributions and express our sincere appreciation for your help.

APPENDIX

These documents and more can be viewed at **wbp.bz/wngallery**

KATHRYN E. LANDRETH
United States Attorney
KURT P. SCHULKE
Attorney in Charge
ERIC JOHNSON
Assistant United States Attorney
Organized Crime Strike Force
United States Attorney's Office
701 East Bridger Avenue, Suite 550
Las Vegas, Nevada 89101
702-388-6363

FILED

JUL 13 1998

CLERK, U.S. DISTRICT COURT
DISTRICT OF NEVADA
BY_____DEPUTY

UNITED STATES DISTRICT COURT

DISTRICT OF NEVADA

-o0o-

UNITED STATES OF AMERICA,
 	
              Plaintiff,
 	
        v.
 	
CHRISTIANO DeCARLO, also known as
    Chris DeCarlo,
MARIO STEFANO, also known as
    Mario Pugliese,
ANTON NELSEN,
KENNETH BYRNES, and
JOSHUA SNELLINGS, also known as
    Josh Snellings,
 	
_____Defendants.
	CR-S-98-375 (PMP)(RLH)
	
	INDICTMENT for Violation of
	Title 18, United States
	Code, Sections 1951,
	Interference with Commerce
	by Threat of Violence (Hobbs
	Act); 1952, Interstate Travel
	in Aid of Racketeering
	Activity; 924(c) Possession of
	Firearm During a Crime of
	Violence; 371, Conspiracy;
	and 2, Aiding and Abetting

THE GRAND JURY CHARGES THAT:

COUNT ONE
(Interference with Commerce by Threats or Violence and Aiding and Abetting)

1.   At all or part of the time material to this Indictment, Frank Bartello, Richard Soranno and Harry Jacobs directly or indirectly owned and operated out call services in the Las Vegas, Nevada, area for the purpose of providing female and male entertainers to individuals in exchange for money, which businesses affected interstate commerce.

1

18

2. At all or part of the time material to this Indictment, defendant **CHRISTIANO DeCARLO** directly or indirectly owned and operated an out call service in the Las Vegas, Nevada, area for the purpose of providing female and male entertainers to individuals in exchange for money, which business affected interstate commerce. Defendant **CHRISTIANO DeCARLO**'s out call service competed for customers with Frank Bartello's, Richard Soranno's and Harry Jacobs' out call services in the Las Vegas, Nevada, area.

3. At all or part of the time material to this Indictment, defendants perceived Charles Coveney as an individual who worked for one or more out call businesses in the Las Vegas, Nevada, area and who, through use of computers and computer networks, was capable of controlling the Sprint telephone system in southern Nevada, which telephone system affected interstate commerce, to divert telephone calls from defendant **CHRISTIANO DeCARLO**'s and other individuals' out call services to Richard Soranno's and possibly other competitor's out call services for the purpose of diverting customers from defendant **CHRISTIANO DeCARLO**'s and other individuals' out call services to Richard Soranno's and possibly other competitor's out call services.

4. From on or about June 1998, through and including the date of this Indictment, in the District of Nevada and elsewhere,

> **CHRISTIANO DeCARLO**, also known as
> Chris DeCarlo,
> **MARIO STEFANO**, also known as
> Mario Pugliese,
> **ANTON NELSEN**,
> **KENNETH BYRNES**, and
> **JOSHUA SNELLINGS**, also known as
> Josh Snellings,

2

defendants herein, and VINCENT CONGIUSTI, who is not charged in this Indictment, and others known and unknown, did conspire to obstruct, delay and affect commerce and the movement of articles in commerce by extortion (as the terms "commerce" and "extortion" are defined in and by Section 1951(b) of Title 18, United States Code) in that defendants did conspire to obtain property, that is, money, from Frank Bartello, Richard Soranno and Harry Jacobs and their out call service businesses and to take ownership and control of Frank Bartello's, Richard Soranno's and Harry Jacobs' out call service businesses, by the wrongful use of threatened and actual force, violence and fear, including threatening of violent crimes and committing violent crimes.

All in violation of Title 18, United States Code, Sections 1951 and 2.

COUNT TWO
(Interstate Travel in Aid of Racketeering Activity and Aiding and Abetting)

3.   On or about October 7, 1998, in the District of Nevada and elsewhere,

CHRISTIANO DeCARLO, also known as
Chris DeCarlo,
MARIO STEFANO, also known as
Mario Pugliese,
ANTON NELSEN,
KENNETH BYRNES, and
JOSHUA SNELLINGS, also known as
Josh Snellings,

the defendants herein, did travel and caused travel in interstate commerce, that is interstate travel from the State of Florida to in or about Las Vegas, Nevada, by VINCENT CONGIUSTI, with the intent to otherwise promote, manage, establish, carry on, or facilitate the

3

promotion, management, establishment, or carrying on of an unlawful
activity, said unlawful activity being extortion in violation of
Nevada Revised Statute Section 205.320 and extortion in violation of
Title 18, United States Code, Section 1951, and thereafter did
perform and attempt to perform acts to promote, manage and carry on
and facilitate the promotion, management and carrying on of said
unlawful activity.

All in violation of Title 18, United States Code, Sections
1952(a)(3) and 2.

COUNT THREE
(Interstate Travel in Aid of Racketeering Activity
and Aiding and Abetting)

4.   On or about October 7, 1998, in the District of Nevada
and elsewhere,

CHRISTIANO DeCARLO, also known as
Christ DeCarlo,
MARIO STEFANO, also known as
Mario Pugliese,
ANTON NELSEN,
KENNETH BYRNES, and
JOSHUA SNELLINGS, also known as
Josh Snellings,

the defendants herein, did travel and caused travel in interstate
commerce, that is interstate travel from the State of Florida to in
or about Las Vegas, Nevada, by defendant ANTON NELSEN, with the
intent to otherwise promote, manage, establish, carry on, or
facilitate the promotion, management, establishment, or carrying on
of an unlawful activity, said unlawful activity being extortion in
violation of Nevada Revised Statute Section 205.320 and extortion in
violation of Title 18, United States Code, Section 1951, and
thereafter did perform and attempt to perform acts to promote,

4

manage and carry on and facilitate the promotion, management and carrying on of said unlawful activity.

All in violation of Title 18, United States Code, Sections 1952(a)(3) and 2.

COUNT FOUR
(Interstate Travel in Aid of Racketeering Activity
and Aiding and Abetting)

5.   On or about October 1, 1998, in the District of Nevada and elsewhere,

CHRISTIANO DeCARLO, also known as
Chris DeCarlo,
MARIO STEFANO, also known as
Mario Pugliese,
ANTON NELSEN,
KENNETH BYRNES, and
JOSHUA SNELLINGS, also known as
Josh Snellings,

the defendants herein, did travel and caused travel in interstate commerce, that is interstate travel from the State of New Jersey to in or about Las Vegas, Nevada, by defendant **KENNETH BYRNES**, with the intent to otherwise promote, manage, establish, carry on, or facilitate the promotion, management, establishment, or carrying on of an unlawful activity, said unlawful activity being extortion in violation of Nevada Revised Statute Section 205.320 and extortion in violation of Title 18, United States Code, Section 1951, and thereafter did perform and attempt to perform acts to promote, manage and carry on and facilitate the promotion, management and carrying on of said unlawful activity.

All in violation of Title 18, United States Code, Sections 1952(a)(3) and 2.

5

COUNT FIVE
(Conspiracy to Commit an Offense Against
the United States)

6.   From in or about June 1998, and continuing up to and including October 13, 1998, in the District of Nevada and elsewhere,

CHRISTIANO DeCARLO, also known as
Chris DeCarlo,
MARIO STEFANO, also known as
Mario Pugliese,
ANTON NELSEN,
KENNETH BYRNES, and
JOSHUA SNELLINGS, also known as
Josh Snellings,

the defendants herein, and VINCENT CONGIUSTI, who is not charged in this Indictment, and others known and unknown to the Grand Jury, did willfully and knowingly combine, conspire, confederate and agree together and with each other to travel and cause travel in interstate commerce to otherwise promote, manage, establish, carry on, or facilitate the promotion, management, establishment, or carrying on of an unlawful activity, said unlawful activity being extortion in violation of Nevada Revised Statute Section 205.320 and extortion in violation of Title 18, United States Code, Section 1951, and thereafter did perform and attempt to perform acts to promote, manage and carry on and facilitate the promotion, management and carrying on of said unlawful activity, in violation of Title 18, United States Code, Section 1952(a)(3).

OVERT ACTS

7.   In furtherance of the above-described conspiracy, the defendants committed the following overt acts:

a.   In or about August 1998, defendant **CHRISTIANO DeCARLO** met with a special agent of the Federal Bureau of Investigation acting

6

1 in an undercover capacity. Defendant **CHRISTIANO DeCARLO** explained
2 to the undercover agent that in the near future individuals would be
3 sent out to the Las Vegas, Nevada, area to extort out call services
4 operators through threats of violence and possibly violence.

5   b.   On or about September 26, 1998, defendant **MARIO STEFANO**
6 spoke over the telephone with Anthony Nastasi. Defendant **MARIO**
7 **STEFANO** advised he was sending someone to Las Vegas to assist
8 defendant **CHRISTIANO DeCARLO**.

9   c.   On or about October 1, 1998, defendant **KENNETH BYRNES**
10 traveled from the outside the State of Nevada to the Las Vegas,
11 Nevada, area;

12   d.   On or about October 5, 1998, defendant **MARIO STEFANO**
13 met with a special agent of the Federal Bureau of Investigation
14 acting in an undercover capacity and Anthony Nastasi. Defendant
15 **MARIO STEFANO** advised that he was sending two individuals from the
16 Tampa, Florida area to the Las Vegas, Nevada area to assist
17 defendant **KENNETH BYRNES** in dealing with Frank Bartello, Richard
18 Serrano, Harry Jacobs, and Charles Coveney.

19   e.   On or about October 5, 1998, defendants **KENNETH BYRNES**
20 and **JOSHUA SNELLINGS** picked up a special agent of the Federal Bureau
21 of the Investigation acting in an undercover capacity at McCarran
22 International Airport, Las Vegas, Nevada. Defendant **KENNETH BYRNES**
23 requested the undercover agent find addresses for individuals in the
24 out call service business before the two men from the Tampa,
25 Florida, area arrived in the Las Vegas, Nevada, area on October 7,
26 1998.

    f.   On or about October 5, 1998, defendant **JOSHUA SNELLINGS**

7 .

1 drove with defendant KENNETH BYRNES and cased an out call business
2 operated by Anthony Cecola's.

3   g.   On or about October 7, 1998, defendant ANTON NELSEN and
4 VINCENT CONGIUSTI traveled from the State of Florida to the Las
5 Vegas, Nevada, area;

6   h.   On October 8, 1998, defendant KENNETH BYRNES spoke with
7 a special agent of the Federal Bureau of Investigation acting in an
8 undercover capacity. Defendant KENNETH BYRNES advised he was in the
9 company of defendant ANTON NELSEN and VINCENT CONGIUSTI and they
10 intended to contact Charles Coveney, take Coveney to an undisclosed
11 location and convince him to assist defendant CHRISTIANO DeCARLO in
12 diverting telephone calls from other out call services to defendant
13 CHRISTIANO DeCARLO's out call business.

14   i.   On or about October 9, 1998, defendants KENNETH BYRNES
15 and ANTON NELSEN and VINCENT CONGIUSTI drove to Frank Bartello's out
16 call service business location at 5030 Paradise Road, Unit B112, Las
17 Vegas, Nevada.

18   j.   On or about October 9, 1998, defendants CHRISTIANO
19 DeCARLO and KENNETH BYRNES spoke over the telephone about how to
20 locate and intercept individuals who were the targets of the
21 extortion. Defendant CHRISTIANO DeCARLO indicated that he would
22 send defendant JOSHUA SNELLINGS to a location to watch for and
23 attempt to locate Charles Coveney.

24   k.   On or about October 9, 1998, defendants ANTON NELSEN and
25 CHRISTIANO DeCARLO and VINCENT CONGIUSTI met with Phil Bunin at the
26 DeCarlo Group offices, 1515 East Tropicana, Unit 640, Las Vegas,
   Nevada.

                              8

All in violation of Title 18, United States Code, Section 371.

COUNT SIX
(Possession of Firearm During Crime of Violence)

On or about October 9, 1998, in the District of Nevada and elsewhere,

CHRISTIANO DeCARLO, also known as
Chris DeCarlo,
MARIO STEFANO, also known as
Mario Pugliese,
ANTON NELSEN,
KENNETH BYRNES, and
JOSHUA SNELLINGS, also known as
Josh Snellings,

defendants herein, did during and in relation to a crime of violence for which they may be prosecuted in a Court of the United States, to wit, conspiracy to interfere with commerce through extortion, as further described in Count One of the Indictment, said count incorporated herein by reference, and interstate travel in furtherance of extortion, as further described in Counts Two through Four of the Indictment, said counts incorporated herein by reference, and conspiracy to engage in interstate travel in furtherance of extortion, as further described in Count Five of the Indictment, said count incorporated herein by reference, did knowingly use and carry a firearm, and, in furtherance of the crime

. . .

. . .

. . .

. . .

. . .

. . .

9

of violence described in this Count of the Indictment, did possess a firearm.

All in violation of Title 18, United States Code, Sections 924(c)

A TRUE BILL:

DATED this 13th day of July, 1999.

_____
FOREPERSON OF THE GRAND JURY

_____
KATHRYN E. LANDRETH
United States Attorney

_____
KURT F. SCHULKE
Chief, Criminal Division and
    Organized Crime Strike Force Unit

_____
ERIC JOHNSON
Assistant United States Attorney
Organized Crime Strike Force Unit

10

United States District Court

DISTRICT OF NEVADA

In the Matter of the Search of
(Name, address or brief description of person or property to be searched)

IN RE: SEARCH WARRANT OF PREMISES KNOWN
AS 3869 ALMONDWOOD DRIVE, LAS VEGAS, NEVADA

SEARCH WARRANT

CASE NUMBER:

MAG. 98-1207-M-RJJ

TO: ANY SPECIAL AGENT
OF THE FEDERAL BUREAU OF INVESTIGATION _____ and any Authorized Officer of the United States.

Affidavit(s) having been made before me by ___Charles Maurer, Special Agent, FBI___ who has reason to
Affiant

believe that ☐ on the person of or ☐ on the premises known as (name, description and/or location)

SEE ATTACHMENT A

in the District of Nevada there is now concealed a certain person or property, namely (describe the person or property)

SEE ATTACHMENT B

I am satisfied that the affidavit(s) attached hereto and incorporated herein establishes probable cause to believe that the person or property so described is now concealed on the person or premises above-described and establish grounds for the issuance of this warrant.

YOU ARE HEREBY COMMANDED to search on or before ___October 19, 1998___
Date

(not to exceed 10 days) the person or place named above for the person or property specified, serving this warrant and making the search (in the daytime - 6:00 A.M. to 10:00 P.M.) (at any time in the day or night as I find reasonable cause has been established) and if the person or property be found there to seize same, leaving a copy of this warrant and receipt for the person or property taken, and prepare a written inventory of the person or property seized and promptly return this to ___LLOYD D. GEORGE, United States District Judge___ U.S. Judge or Magistrate
as required by law.

_____ at ___Las Vegas, Nevada___
Date and Time Issued   City and State

LLOYD D. GEORGE
United States District Judge
Name and Title of Judicial Officer   Signature of Judicial Officer

Attachment A

<u>CHRISTIANO DeCARLO RESIDENCE</u>
Christiano DeCarlo resides at 3869 Almondwood, Las Vegas, Nevada. DeCarlo's residence is described as a an offwhite stucco two story single family dwelling with dark brown trim, two car garage and the numbers 3869 on the curb in front of the house.

Attachment B

1.   Handguns of any caliber and shotguns of any caliber, and ammunition for any handgun or shotgun, and any miscellaneous gun pieces, gun-cleaning items or kits, holsters, ammunition belts, original packaging, targets, expended pieces of lead, any photographs of firearms, and any paperwork showing the purchase, storage, disposition, or dominion and control over any guns, any ammunition, or any of the above items.

2.   Any documentation, notes, drawings, maps, or recordation or diagrams relating to the customs or habits, associated with Coveney, Saranno, Bartello and Ceccola and out call businesses in Las Vegas area, including phone numbers, addresses, listing of street names or names of locations and places frequented by Coveney, Saranno, Bartello and Ceccola, noted descriptions of vehicles used by Coveney, Saranno, Bartello and Ceccola, notations of times of day or night significant to the schedule of Coveney, Serono, Bartello and Ceccolo, notations of individuals close to or associated with Coveney, Soranno, Bartello and Ceccola and out call businesses in the Las Vegas area.

3.   Carburetor cleaner, destructive devices, accelerant, fuses, blasting caps, PVC caps, black powder, PVC piping and tape.

4.   Airline tickets, car rental agreements, hotel room receipts and registration documents and other documents evidencing travel.

5.   Cellular telephones

6.   Phone bills and business records from January 1997 to the present showing telephone calls to or from specific locations or telephones.

7.   Bank or other financial institution records reflecting any deposits or withdrawal activity on bank accounts from January 1997 to the present.

8.   Records from January 1997 to present of payments of sums of money, purchase of money orders or cashier checks, and loan documents and lien documents.

9.   Daily logs, daily telephone diaries, general diaries or journals and appointment calendars;

10.   Address books and rolodex type address systems and lists or notes containing addresses, numbers, telephone numbers, license numbers and names;

11.   Exemplars of original handwriting including signature cards, usage cards and applications, negotiable instruments;

1

12. Personal computers, automated data processing systems, compatible floppy or fixed disk drives, tape or optical drives, necessary to access any of the above records.

13. Any telephone answering device or machine and/or any recording tapes located therein.

14. Any articles of personal property tending to establish the identity of persons who have dominion and control over the premises to be searched, including rent receipts, utility bills, telephone bills, addressed mail, personal identification, keys, purchase receipts, sales receipts, photographs, vehicle pink slips and vehicle registration;

15. knifes and rope

2

STATE OF NEVADA)
) ss:
COUNTY OF CLARK)

AFFIDAVIT FOR SEARCH WARRANT

I, Charles Maurer, Special Agent, Federal Bureau of Investigation, having been duly sworn, state:

I am a case agent for a federal grand jury investigation of **Christiano DeCarlo, Kenneth P. Burns, Vincent Congiusti, and Anton Nelson, Josh Snellings** and others known and unknown for alleged criminal violations of Title 18 and Title 26, United States Code. I have been a special agent with the Federal Bureau of Investigation for 23 years. I have been assigned to the Organized Crime Squad of the Las Vegas Office of the FBI for the last 3 years. During the course of my work I have been involved in numerous investigations concerning violations of Title 18, United States Code, Sections 1962(c) and (d), RICO (and corresponding state law predicate violations including murder), 1958, Use of Interstate Facilities for Murder for Hire, 1959, Violence in Furtherance of Racketeering Enterprise, 1951, Interference in Commerce by Threats of Violence, and 2315, Receipt of Stolen Property. I have worked with other law enforcement officers on both the state and federal levels concerning investigations of extortion, murder for hire and murder and various firearms related offenses. I consequently am thoroughly familiar with the manner and means in which extortion is committed.

Based on my training and experience as a Special Agent, my personal participation in this investigation, and from reports made

1

to me by fellow Special Agents of the Federal Bureau of Investigation, I allege the facts contained in the paragraphs below and the attached affidavit, incorporated herein by reference, show that:

A. There is probable cause to believe that **Christiano DeCarlo, Kenneth P. Burns, Vincent Congiusti,** and **Anton Nelson, Josh Snellings** and others known and unknown are:

1) affecting and attempting and conspiring to affect interstate commerce by extortion in violation of 18 U.S.C § 1951.

2) traveling in interstate commerce to commit a crime of violence in furtherance of extortion in violation of Nevada Revised Statute Section 205.320 and Title 18, United States Code, Section 1951, in violation of 18 U.S.C. 1952.

3) conspiracy to violate 18 U.S.C. 1952, in violation of 18 U.S.C. 371.

B. There is probable cause to believe that

I have probable cause to believe that evidence of these crimes is now concealed on the premises known as:

1. Business Offices for DeCarlo Group and Argot Appropriations, 1515 East Tropicana, Units 640 and 642, Las Vegas, Nevada;

2. 1996 Ford Expedition, White Color, Nevada License Plate Number 122GUL;

3. 1998 Ford Expedition, Green Color, Nevada License Plate Number 667HXY; and

4. Residence of Christiano DeCarlo, 3869 Almondwood Drive, Las Vegas, Nevada.

These locations and individuals will be more particularly described in this affidavit.

2

STATEMENT OF FACTS

8. This investigation was predicated upon information received from numerous sources which indicate that a significant portion of the out call business in Las Vegas, also known as the escort service business, is merely a front for money laundering, robbery, prostitution, narcotics distribution, and other criminal activity. Out call services are legal in the State of Nevada and are licensed by Clark County. An out call service sends male and female dancers, referred to as entertainers, to customers who are usually in hotel rooms. The customer pays a fee, usually between $150.00 and $200.00, which is split between the agency and the entertainer. Many out call agencies operate within the law, but a few engage in the various illegal activities described in this affidavit. In addition, these same sources referred to above have advised that the LCN is making an attempt to gain control of this lucrative cash business through threats, extortion, and other illegal means. Allegations have also been made that certain out call service operators have made cash payments and given gifts or favors to members of local law enforcement in return for protection from arrest and that there are one or more individuals in the Clark County District Attorney's Office that may have been compromised. Other illegal activity has been alleged, such as the use of electronic means to divert calls from competitors' businesses and the use of the out call businesses to launder money.

9. In November of 1997, the Las Vegas Division of the Federal Bureau of Investigation (FBI) was contacted by an individual who was formerly a cooperating witness (herein after referred to as CW-1) for the New York Division of the FBI. CW-1 has assisted the FBI in the

3

past and has portrayed himself as someone who is connected to the LCN in New York. CW-1 advised that he operates out call services in New York and Las Vegas and that he had been arrested while in Las Vegas. CW-1 asserted that he was not engaging in illegal activity and that he believed that the arrest was merely a retaliation for his attempt to expand into the Las Vegas area. After his arrest, CW-1 was kicked several times by one of the arresting officers in an area near the jail which is out of view of the surveillance cameras and he was warned that he "needed to learn how we do business in Las Vegas."

10. Shortly after his release, CW-1 was contacted by an individual named Christiano DeCarlo, who was previously unknown to the CW-1. DeCarlo claimed that he is connected to Vincent Faraci and John Conti, both of whom are known to the FBI as members of the LCN, and that DeCarlo could help CW-1 with the pending charges. Faraci is the son of John Faraci, also known as Johnny Green, who is an acting capo in the Bonanno LCN family. Faraci is known to have recently borrowed $100,000 from John Gotti, Jr., and it also appears from investigations conducted by the FBI that the Gambino LCN family is behind the attempt to gain control of the Las Vegas out call industry. Investigation determined that DeCarlo is also an out call service operator in Las Vegas. CW-1 agreed to assist the FBI in this investigation and to permit the FBI to place an undercover FBI agent (UCA) to pose as an employee of his Las Vegas business.

11. Previous investigations of the out call business by the FBI and local law enforcement have focused primarily on the act of prostitution rather than on the individuals who operate the business. These investigations have had little success because those out call

4

service operators who operate illegally shield themselves from prosecution by claims of ignorance as to the prostitution and other illegal activities. In addition, investigations focusing on prostitution have little jury appeal because prostitution is legal in many areas of Nevada, although not in Las Vegas. Consequently, a decision was made to initiate an undercover operation (UCO) which would target not prostitution, but those crimes traditionally associated with the LCN such as extortion, murder, and money laundering.

12. In June of 1998, a meeting was arranged between DeCarlo, CW-1, and the UCA. During this conversation, DeCarlo detailed his involvement in the out call business and agreed to assist the CW in "fixing" his pending case. DeCarlo told CW-1 to return to New York and await contact from someone there. Shortly after returning to New York, CW-1 was contacted by an individual who identified himself as "Mario." Mario has been identified as Mario Pugliesi, a Gambino LCN family associate. Pugliesi arranged a meeting with CW-1 during which he agreed to assist the CW-1 with his case if CW-1 "check out." In the meantime, the UCA contacted Vincent Faraci in Las Vegas. Faraci told the UCA that he would do business with the UCA later if everything checked out and a formal introduction was made by the right people.

13. In early August of 1998, CW-1 was again contacted by Pugliesi in New York. Pugliesi told CW-1 that he had looked into the CW-1's background and he was now prepared to deal with him. Another meeting between CW-1 and Pugliesi was set for August 17, 1998. During this meeting, Pugliesi stated that he could assist CW-1 in fixing his

5

case but the cost to CW-1 would be $25,000. After some negotiation by CW-1 Pugliesi agreed to accept $10,000, which Pugliesi claimed would cover only the "costs" of taking care of CW-1's case. Pugliesi also stated that he could arrange to increase the amount of business at CW-1's Las Vegas out call service in return for a share of the profits. CW-1 complained to Pugliesi about some of his competitors in Las Vegas, namely Frank Bartello and Richard Soxanno. Pugliesi replied that he was aware of both of those individuals and that "a couple aspirins will be sent to Las Vegas to deal with those headaches."

14. The meetings between Pugliesi and CW-1 were surveilled by agents of the New York Office of the FBI. Pugliesi told CW-1 that he used to be "with Roy DeMeo," who was a Gambino LCN family capo with a reputation for violence. DeMeo is now deceased. Pugliesi added that the people with whom he is now connected are "crazier than DeMeo."

15. After consideration of the severity of the criminal activity and the potential for violence by the subjects, FBI authority was obtained to make the $10,000 payment. Consequently, on August 20, 1998, the UCA met with DeCarlo and paid the $10,000. A lengthy consensually recorded conversation took place during this meeting in which DeCarlo discussed the plans that he and Pugliesi had made in regard to the future of the out call business in Las Vegas. DeCarlo stated that he had been working on behalf of Pugliesi for about a year and a half and that he had checked out all the major players in the out call business, particularly to determine if they had any LCN affiliations with other cities. DeCarlo told the UCA that he had

6

hesitated to help CW-1 because he was afraid of risking any "heat" at this very crucial time, but that he had agreed because Pugliesi said that there could be long term advantages. DeCarlo stated that in the near future individuals would be sent to deal with Bartello, Soranno, and another unnamed out call service operator. They would each be given a choice between giving over control of their businesses to DeCarlo or being killed. DeCarlo stated that he persuaded Pugliesi not to kill all three at one time because, although such a crime might go unnoticed in New York City, the death of three out call service operators in Las Vegas in a short period of time would call attention to them. DeCarlo told the UCA that Las Vegas is not used to this type of activity, referring to the proposed murders.

16. In a subsequent meeting between the UCA and DeCarlo on August 20, 1998, DeCarlo reviewed CW-1's case file relating to the charges pending against CW-1. The UCA had obtained the file from the CW-1's attorney at DeCarlo's request. After reviewing the file, DeCarlo placed a call to a local attorney, Glen Lerner, and arranged a three-week continuance of CW-1's case. Later, CW-1 spoke with Lerner by telephone and met with him in person. Lerner confirmed that he intended to get the case fixed for CW-1 and that the continuance was necessary to allow DeCarlo to do what he had to do to get the case fixed. Lerner also bragged to CW-1 that his father had served time for murder. Investigation determined that Lerner's father is Pro Lerner, who is connected to the LCN in the Boston area and had served 15 years in New York on a murder conviction.

17. On September 9, 1998, a second CW (referred to herein as CW-2) advised that he has been in contact with members of the Rolling

7

60's gang in Los Angeles and that two members of the gang had been hired by DeCarlo to murder one of DeCarlo's competitors, Anthony Ceccola. CW-2 has been a source of the FBI for approximately 2 years. CW-2 has made consensual recordings and has introduced undercover agents to various subjects. CW-2 has proven to provided reliable information. CW-2 has consensually recorded conversations between himself and Daniel Slaughter and between himself, Slaughter and DeCarlo.

Ceccola is connected to the Philadelphia LCN family and he operates several out call services in Las Vegas. Ceccola had recently expanded his operation into Atlantic City, New Jersey. It is unknown if this expansion is the cause of the retaliation by DeCarlo, although DeCarlo did advise the UCA that Ceccola is a "punk" and that the UCA should not worry about him.

CW-2 informed the FBI on September 9, 1998, that two members of the Rolling 60's, Daniel Slaughter (also known as "Icon") and Darren Lowery, had come to Las Vegas during the week of September 1, 1998, for the purpose of killing Ceccola. The FBI was unaware of this activity before being advised by CW-2 on September 9, 1998. CW-2 said that Slaughter told him that he and Lowery stayed at DeCarlo's residence. I have reviewed telephone subscriber records and determined that DeCarlo's residence in 3869 Almondwood, Las Vegas, Nevada. I have also determined that DeCarlo has an American West frequent flyer membership using 3869 Almondwood address. Slaughter and Lowery conducted extensive surveillance of Ceccola, but were unable to find an opportunity to kill him. During the course of their activities in Las Vegas, Slaughter and Lowery were involved in a hit

8

and run accident. Due to the fact that their car had been observed and they had several weapons in the car, Slaughter and Lowery decided to return to Los Angeles. CW-2 has stated that Slaughter intends to return to Las Vegas to kill Ceccola in the near future. Ceccola has been advised by the FBI of the threat on his life. CW-2 has also stated that the introduction of DeCarlo to Slaughter was made by Kevin Rowe, who is a paralegal working for attorney Glen Lerner.

On or about October 5 or 6, 1998, CW-2 stated that Slaughter and requested to obtain a 45 caliber pistol. Slaughter informed CW-2 that he had been contacted by his man in Las Vegas (DeCarlo) and he was going to complete the work he had gone to Las Vegas to do before (kill Ceccola). Slaughter said he had three other guns and body armor for one individual. The FBI warned Ceccola again of the threat on his life and agents understand that Ceccola left Las Vegas.

On or about October 6 and 7, 1998, CW-2 advised that Slaughter contacted him and told him Chris DeCarlo was sending him to San Diego, California, to kill an unnamed individual for DeCarlo.

18. On September 26, 1998, during a consensually monitored telephone call between Pugliesi and CW-1, Pugliesi advised he is sending someone to Las Vegas to assist DeCarlo in case he needs to "bang heads."

19. On September 29, 1998, during a consensually monitored telephone conversation between Pugliesi and CW-1, Pugliesi advised he is sending two other individuals to Las Vegas to assist the individual he referred to in the September 26, 1998, phone call. Pugliesi further identified this individual "Kenny," last name not given. Pugliesi said Kenny and the two other individuals will "deal with"

9

Soranno, Jacobs and one other individual, all of whom are owners of out call services.

20. Later on September 29, 1998, Kenny (later identified as Kenneth P. Byrnes) and CW-1 had a telephone conversation. During this conversation Byrnes advised he will travel to Las Vegas and "persuade" owners of out call services to cooperate with DeCarlo. 21. On October 1, 1998, during a consensually monitored telephone call between Pugliesi and CW-1, Pugliesi advised that he was sending people from Tampa, Florida, to Las Vegas to assist Byrnes in dealing with the previously identified owners of out call businesses.

22. On October 5, 1998, CW-1 received a message in CW-1's telephone paging device to contact telephone number (702) 682-3881. CW telephoned this number and it was answered by Kenneth P. Byrnes. Byrnes advised he was in Las Vegas and was to be joined by two individuals from Tampa, Florida, who would assist him. These individuals were scheduled to arrive on October 7, 1998, in the morning.

23. Later on October 5, 1998, CW-1 contacted Byrnes at (702) 682-3881, and requested Byrnes to meet UCA at the Las Vegas airport at 10:00 p.m. on October 5, 1998.

24. At approximately 10:00 p.m on October 5, 1998, UCA met Byrnes at the Las Vegas airport and was driven by Byrnes and another individual identified as Josh (Last Name Unknown) from the airport to the UCA's resident. The UCA was wearing a hidden body recorder at this time. Byrnes advised that individuals from Tampa, Florida, were arriving on October 7, 1998, and intended to meet with and possibly make an example of one of the previously described owners of out call

10

services.

25. On October 5, 1998, UCA and CW-1 met Pugliesi in New York City. CW-1 was wearing a hidden body recorder during this meeting. Pugliesi advised he is sending two individuals from Tampa, Florida, to Las Vegas, Nevada, to assist Byrnes in dealing with Bartello, Soranno, and Jacobs, all of whom are out call service operators. Pugliesi advised one of the individuals coming to Las Vegas is known as "Vinnie Aspirins" and the other is a former mercenary. Pugliesi said that Vinnie "Aspirins" has a reputation for torturing people. Pugliesi advised on one occasion Vinnie "Aspirins" used a cordless drill to drill holes into an individual's head.

26. On or about October 5, 1998, Pugliesi told CW-1 that in addition to the out call business operators targeted, he has targeted an individual named Charles Coveney. Pugliesi said that Coveney is a computer expert who currently works for Soranno. Coveney has contacts in the Sprint Telephone Company and is able to have telephone calls diverted from one number to another. Pugliesi expects to persuade Coveney to leave Soranno and assist DeCarlo in his out call business by diverting telephone calls to DeCarlo.

On or about October 5, 1998, during a meeting between CW-1, UCA and Pugliesi, Pugliesi advised that he was involved in a cigarette smuggling operation in the Bahamas. In an attempt to raise money for this smuggling operation, Pugliesi and his associates from Tampa Florida, met with an unnamed individual and "persuaded" him against his will to sign over a $300,000 lien on a hotel he owns in the Bahamas. The lien was made in the name of Christiano DeCarlo and was to be used by DeCarlo to obtain a $300,000 loan.

11

On October 5, 1998, Byrnes and Josh Snellings picked up the UCA at the airport in Las Vegas. Brynes requested the UCA to find addresses for individuals. Brynes told the UCA to find the addresses before the people from Tampa arrived in Las Vegas on October 7, 1998. Brynes indicated that Vinnie Aspirins was a torturer who was a feared killer and said that the other man from Tampa was an explosive expert. After the UCA was dropped off, surveillance observed Snellings drive Brynes to Ceccola's out call business.

Brynes on one occasion indicated to the UCA that he relied on Snellings to drive him around Las Vegas.

During the week of October 5, 1998, CW-2 stated that he had been requested by DeCarlo, Kevin Rowe and Glenn Lerner to provide addresses for Coveney and others.

27. On October 6, 1998, UCA met Byrnes and DeCarlo at DeCarlo's office, 1515 Tropicana Avenue, Las Vegas, Nevada. During this meeting Byrnes identified the two individuals coming from Tampa, Florida, as "Vinnie" and "Anton." Byrnes advised that these individuals would be arriving at 8:50 a.m. on October 7, 1998.

28. At approximately 8:50 a.m. special agents of the FBI observed Vincent Congiusti and Anton Nelson depart a flight from Tampa, Florida, arriving at the Las Vegas airport.

29. Congiusti and Nelson were observed meeting Byrnes and leaving the airport in a 1998 Ford Expedition bearing Nevada license plate number 667 HXY.

30. During the morning of October 7, 1998, the UCA telephonically contacted Byrnes. During this conversation Byrnes requested the UCA's assistance in determining home addresses of Frank

12

"Vince" Bartello, Richard Soranno, and Harry Jacobs. Byrnes advised he was in Room 1860 at the Alexis Park Resort Hotel, Las Vegas, Nevada. The UCA advised he would recontact Byrnes.

31. Also during the morning of October 7, 1998, CW-1 telephonically contacted Byrnes. Byrnes advised he was in the company of Vinnie and the other individual from Tampa. Byrnes put Congiusti on the telephone with CW-1. Congiusti advised CW-1 that they expect to make contact with out call service operators and he expects that one of them will "go bang." CW-1 believes this means that Congiusti and the others plan to blow up someone's office. CW-1 stated that Pugliesi told him on a previous occasion that Vinnie's partner blew up his dentist's office because he was angry with the dentist.

32. Congiusti, Nelson, and Byrnes were under physical surveillance by FBI agents during October 7, 1998, and October 8, 1998. During this time period Congiusti, Nelson, and Byrnes were observed to meet with Christiano DeCarlo on at least five occasions. Two of the meetings occurred at DeCarlo's place of business and one occurred in a hotel room at the Alexis Park Resort Hotel, Las Vegas, Nevada. The meeting at the hotel included the above four individuals and another unknown individual. The unknown individual was observed carrying a suitcase into the hotel room and leaving without it.

33. During a physical surveillance on October 7, 1998, Congiusti, Nelson, and Byrnes were observed in the above described 1998 Ford Expedition in the vicinity of 900 East Karen Avenue, Las Vegas, Nevada. This address is the business address of Richard Soranno.

34. On October 8, 1998, Special Agents of the FBI observed

13

Congiusti and Nelson in a room at the Alexis Park Hotel beginning at 11:30 a.m. They were joined by Christiano DeCarlo at 2:10 p.m. and as of 2:20 p.m. all three were together in the room. 35. On October 8, 1998, Special Agents of the FBI reviewed records at the Alexis Park Resort Hotel, Las Vegas, Nevada, those records reflect Room 1860 and Room 1862 are registered to Christiano DeCarlo. Hotel records indicate a departure date of October 9, 1998.

36. Special agents of the FBI also contacted officials at America West Airlines. Airline officials advised that Congiusti and Nelson had reservations from Tampa, Florida, to Las Vegas, Nevada, which included a return flight to Tampa, Florida, at 11:50 p.m. on October 9, 1998.

37. On October 8, 1998, UCA telephonically contacted Byrnes at (702) 682-3118. Byrnes advised that he was in the company of the two individuals from Tampa and they had been at the Spy Shop purchasing surveillance equipment. Byrnes further advised that the first individual to be contacted by them would be Charles Coveney. Byrnes said Coveney was a computer expert. Byrnes told the UCA they planned to take Coveney to an undisclosed location and convince him to assist Christiano DeCarlo in diverting telephone calls from other out call services to DeCarlo's out call business. Byrnes requested the UCA to assist in the questioning of Coveney because Byrnes believes the UCA to be a computer expert.

38. Congiusti is currently the subject of an FBI investigation in Tampa, Florida. Congiusti is alleged to have attempted to extort $200,000 from a restaurant owner. During this extortion attempt Congiusti held a gun to the restaurant owner's head. The extortion

14

was thwarted because the restaurant owner was affiliated with the Bonanno LCN family.

CW-2 on October 8, 1998, had a telephone call with DeCarlo and Kevin Rowe. DeCarlo indicated it was essential to find the address for Coveney. DeCarlo explained that three people were in from Tampa and if they did not complete their plans they would come back at a later time.

On October 9, 1998, in the early morning, Congiusti and Nelson discussed the fact that they needed to revisit some of the locations they had previously observed but that Brynes had the map.

On October 9, 1998, 12:59 a.m., a conversation was intercepted between Congest and Nelson in Room 1860 at the Alexis Park Hotel. During the conversation the men commented that they wanted a limo to deliver them to an location. A comment was made that they were not going to hurt someone at the location but they were going to make him think so. Congest said it was too bad Mario (Pugliesi) told the "kid" (DeCarlo) that they had a "badge" (member of the LCN) because now they had to go through with it. They discussed trying to find a house in North west Las Vegas at 6:00 a.m. in the morning and busting down the door. They made the comment that they were going to get the "B guy." They said that Kenny (Byrnes) was stuck on the Coveney deal. They commented that Byrnes was stupid and not cautious.

On October 9, 1998, at approximately 6:28 a.m., in Room 1860, Congest and Nelson were intercepted. They discussed how Kenny (Brynes) is a psychotic and talks too much. They discussed that after they completed this "piece of work," they should also "do" (kill) Kenny. They discussed taking Kenny to practice with the pistol and

15

have an "accidental discharge" on Kenny. On a later conversation on
the same day at 11:54 a.m. Nelson advised Congest that he had brought
the carburetor cleaner. FBI surveillance had earlier the same morning
observe both Nelson and Congest at an auto parts store. I have spoken
to Agent Dennis Passerman who has recently completed bomb technician
school. He advised that carburetor cleaner is highly volatile and can
be used as an accelerant in fire bombings. They also stated that they
would have time to do it after their meeting.

At 12:38 p.m., a telephone conversation was overheard in the Room
1860. Congest told Kenny that he felt Kenny should get out of there.
I believe Congest was referring to DeCarlo's office where Congest and
Nelson subsequently met with DeCarlo. Significantly, when agents
entered DeCarlo's offices, Brynes was found in an adjacent room.
Congest then stated that he had a black bag with more tape, rope, and
the shells. Congest was observed leaving Room 1860 carrying a black
bag which he placed in the Green Ford Expedition, license 667HXY. FBI
surveillance did not observe anyone remove the bag from the Ford
Expedition and it was not found at the scene of the arrest.

On October 7 and 8, 1998, FBI agents observed DeCarlo, Byrnes,
Congest, and Nelson in a 1996 Ford Expedition, License 122GUL, while
in the vehicle the four were observed to drive by 845 Northeastern
Avenue, Las Vegas, Nevada, which they believed to be the address of
Coveney. On October 9, 1998, Congest, Nelson and Byrnes were observed
in a 1998, Green, Ford Expedition, License 667HXY. During the morning
of Oct. 9, 1998, the three were observed to travel to 845 Northeastern
Avenue, Las Vegas, Nevada, which they believed to the address of
Coveney. They were also observed to drive to 5030 Paradise Road, Las

16

Vegas, Nevada. This is the address for an out call business operated by Frank Bartello. While at this location, Nelson was observed exiting the vehicle and walking in the vicinity of B112, which is the unit where Bartello's out call service is located.

Early afternoon on October 9, 1998, Congiusti, Nelson, and Brynes were observed at 1515 East Tropicana, Las Vegas, Unit 640, which is the location of the DeCarlo Group offices and the offices of Chris DeCarlo. A short time later, Nelson and Congiusti left and returned. Subsequently, FBI agents entered DeCarlo's office and discovered Congiusti, Nelson and DeCarlo having threatening conversation with Phil Bunin. Brynes was located in an adjacent office, number 642, with the name ARGOT APPROPRIATIONS.

During an interview by agents, Bunin advised that he was a media consultant. Bunin said he was questioned by DeCarlo and Congest and Nelson regarding his knowledge of individuals in the out call business. Congest was particularly interested in the location of Coveney. The men also questioned Bunin about his knowledge of Richard Soranno, Philip Smith, and Robert Wade. Bunin advised that these men were operators of out call businesses. Bunin said the men demanded Bunin repay a debt of $12,000 or $20,000 to DeCarlo for work a friend of Bunin's failed to do for DeCarlo concerning DeCarlo's computers. Bunin advised that he told the men what he thought they wanted to hear so that he could get out of the office.

At the time of their arrests, Nelson had a handgun and two knifes on his person. Nelson after being advise of his Miranda rights stated to agents that he was a felon. At the current time, agents have been unable to confirm whether Nelson does have a felony conviction.

17

DeCarlo had a semi-automatic pistol within arms reach underneath his desk. Congiusti had a switch-blade knife.

DESIRED SEARCH WARRANTS

Based on the facts in this affidavit I believe that probable cause exists to believe that DeCarlo, Congiusti, Nelson, Brynes, and Josh Snellings participated in a conspiracy to extort Con and owners of Las Vegas out call businesses. I also believe that probable cause exists to believe that certain evidence relevant to the criminal conduct alleged in this affidavit is located at the locations to be searched. Based on my experience and the experience of other law enforcement officers involved in the investigation of extortion, arson, and firearm offenses, the conspirators will have firearms, knifes, rope and other weapons or items used for kidnaping, torture or murder in their vehicles, offices and residences.

In addition to any firearms intended to be used in the extortion, I expect to find and request permission to seize miscellaneous gun pieces, ammunition, gun-cleaning items or kits, holsters, ammunition belts, original box packaging, targets, expended pieces of lead, photographs of firearms, and paperwork showing the purchase, storage, disposition, or dominion and control over guns, ammunition and other above-described items. It is my opinion that above related items would tend to show that firearms existed and had once been located in a place to which the suspects had access, and that these items would tend to connect the suspects with the extortion conspiracy.

According to CW-2, Slaughter indicated that he was in telephonic contact with DeCarlo regarding the Ceccola murder plan and the murder plan in San Diego. Pugliese indicated to CW-1 and UCA that he was in

18

telephone contact with DeCarlo. Brynes indicated that he was in telephone contact with Congiusti and Nelson in Tampa. Brynes requested the UCA to find addresses for Bartello, Soranno, Coveney and Jacobs. DeCarlo requested CW-2 to find addresses, including an address for Coveney. From my experience investigation criminal activity, I know that individuals involved in crime usually keep the names, addresses and telephone numbers of their criminal associates or victims in address books or on note pads or paper sheets. These address book and notes could show a relationship between the suspects and other conspirators. These items could support other evidence indicating the conspirators intended to extort certain victims. Consequently, I request permission to seize address books or records or lists of persons, including names, addresses, phone numbers, notations and notebooks of acquaintances or associates.

From my experience and the experience of other law enforcement officers involved in extortions and planned violent crimes, I know that extorters frequently surveille and observe their intended victims to learn the victim's habits and patterns. Extorters do this to avoid surprise during the actual execution of threats or acts of violence to better ensure the success of the extortion. In conducting this surveillance, contract extorters will often take notes or make drawings or maps or diagrams relating to the customs or habits associated with the victims. Congiusti and Nelson commented that Brynes had a map of various locations. Consequently, I request permission to seize any documentation, notes, drawings, maps, or recordation or diagrams relating to the customs or habits, associated with Coveney, Soranno, Bartello and Ceccola and out call businesses

19

in Las Vegas area, including phone numbers, addresses, listing of street names or names of locations and places frequented by Coveney, Soranno, Bartello and Ceccola, noted descriptions of vehicles used by Coveney, Soranno, Bartello and Ceccola, notations of times of day or night significant to the schedule of Coveney, Soranno, Bartello and Ceccola, notations of individuals close to or associated with Coveney, Soranno, Bartello and Ceccola and out call businesses in the Las Vegas area.

As noted above, DeCarlo provided the conspirators a cellular phone to communicate while they were in Las Vegas. Seizure of the cellular phone from the residences of the subjects would provide significant evidence of the possession of and dominion over the cellular telephone. Seizure of additional telephones would also reveal other telephones available to the subjects for use in coordinating the extortion.

Phone bills and business records from January 1997 to the present showing telephone calls to or from specific locations or telephones. From my experience I am aware that individuals involved in a criminal endeavor typically keep in contact with each other by the telephone.

I also request authority to seize bank records reflecting any deposits or withdrawal activity on bank accounts from January 1997 to the present. I also request authority to seize records of payments of sums of money, purchase of money orders or cashier checks, and loan documents, lien documents. Pugliese has indicated that he and DeCarlo have obtained legitimate loans using extorted collateral (lien documents on a Bahama hotel) to finance illegal activity, specifically cigarette smuggling. From my experience, the subjects may have

20

deposited part of the money from loans in their bank accounts for distribution or use.

I further request permission to seize any articles of personal property tending to establish the identity of persons who have dominion and control over the premises, automobile, or items to be seized, including but not limited to, rent receipts, utility bills, telephone bills, addressed mail, personal identification, keys, purchase receipts, sales receipts, photographs, vehicle pink slips and vehicle registration. I believe that these items will tend to connect the premises, person, locations and vehicles to be searched with the items to be seized and the case being investigated. I believe these items are not the type normally disposed of and will therefore likely be found on the person and at the locations to be searched.

DeCARLO GROUP OFFICES AND ARGOT APPROPRIATIONS OFFICES

DeCarlo Group Offices and Argot Appropriations Offices are located next to each other in Units 640 and 642 at 1515 East Tropicana Avenue, Las Vegas, Nevada, described as a one story office complex located on the south side of Tropicana near the intersection of Tamarus. DeCarlo Group is located in Unit 640 and the door is marked DeCarlo Group and has the number 640 on it. Argot Appropriations is located in Unit 642 and the door is marked with Argot Appropriations and the number 642.

CHRISTIANO DeCARLO RESIDENCE

Christiano DeCarlo resides at 3869 Almondwood, Las Vegas, Nevada. DeCarlo's residence is described as a an offwhite stucco two story single family dwelling with dark brown trim, two car garage and the numbers 3869 on the curb in front of the house.

21

1996 FORD EXPEDITION

1996 Ford Expedition, White Color, Nevada License Plate Number 122GUL.

1998 FORD EXPEDITION

1998 Ford Expedition, Green Color, Nevada License Plate Number 667HXY.

I request authority to search for the following evidence at the residences and vehicles:

1. Handguns of any caliber and shotguns of any caliber, and ammunition for any handgun or shotgun, and any miscellaneous gun pieces, gun-cleaning items or kits, holsters, ammunition belts, original packaging, targets, expended pieces of lead, any photographs of firearms, and any paperwork showing the purchase, storage, disposition, or dominion and control over any guns, any ammunition, or any of the above items.

2. Any documentation, notes, drawings, maps, or recordation or diagrams relating to the customs or habits, associated with Coveney, Saranno, Bartello and Ceccola and out call businesses in Las Vegas area, including phone numbers, addresses, listing of street names or names of locations and places frequented by Coveney, Saranno, Bartello and Ceccola, noted descriptions of vehicles used by Coveney, Saranno, Bartello and Ceccola, notations of times of day or night significant to the schedule of Coveney, Serono, Bartello and Ceccolo, notations of individuals close to or associated with Coveney, Soranno, Bartello and Ceccola and out call businesses in the Las Vegas area.

3. Carburetor cleaner, destructive devices, accelerant, fuses, blasting caps, PVC caps, black powder, PVC piping and tape.

22

4.   Airline tickets, car rental agreements, hotel room receipts and registration documents and other documents evidencing travel.

5.   Cellular telephones

6.   Phone bills and business records from January 1997 to the present showing telephone calls to or from specific locations or telephones.

7.   Bank or other financial institution records reflecting any deposits or withdrawal activity on bank accounts from January 1997 to the present.

8.   Records from January 1997 to present of payments of sums of money, purchase of money orders or cashier checks, and loan documents and lien documents.

9.   Daily logs, daily telephone diaries, general diaries or journals and appointment calendars;

10.   Address books and rolodex type address systems and lists or notes containing addresses, numbers, telephone numbers, license numbers and names;

11.   Exemplars of original handwriting including signature cards, usage cards and applications, negotiable instruments;

12.   Personal computers, automated data processing systems, compatible floppy or fixed disk drives, tape or optical drives, necessary to access any of the above records.

13.   Any telephone answering device or machine and/or any recording tapes located therein.

14.   Any articles of personal property tending to establish the identity of persons who have dominion and control over the premises to be searched, including rent receipts, utility bills, telephone

23

bills, addressed mail, personal identification, keys, purchase receipts, sales receipts, photographs, vehicle pink slips and vehicle registration;

15. knifes and rope

DATE this ____ day of October, 1997.

Charles Maurer
CHARLES MAURER
Special Agent
Federal Bureau of Investigation

SUBSCRIBED and SWORN to before me
this ____ day of October, 1998.

UNITED STATES MAGISTRATE JUDGE

*These documents and more can be
viewed at* **wbp.bz/wngallery**

*For More News About Glen Meek and Dennis
N. Griffin Signup For Our Newsletter:*

http://wbp.bz/newsletter

*Word-of-mouth is critical to an author's long-
term success. If you appreciated this book please
leave a review on the Amazon sales page:*

http://wbp.bz/wna

INTRODUCTION

My name is Joseph Silvestri. My mother called me Joseph, but to most everybody else I was Joe or Joey. I was born in Astoria, Queens, on May 1, 1932, and had five brothers and two sisters. When I was six, we moved to Jackson Heights, also in Queens. We were about the only Italian family there at the time. I'd say I had a normal childhood and was an average or above student.

If I had to name my biggest fault as a kid and young adult, I'd say it was my penchant for using my fists. I was quick to fight and was pretty good at it. I wasn't particularly big, but I packed a wallop that broke some jaws and noses over the years. That talent—if that's the right word—came in handy on some occasions and caused problems other times.

After an abbreviated stint in the US Air Force in 1949, I spent several years working as a bartender or bouncer at various clubs in New York City, including three years at the world-famous Copacabana. I also worked some of the biggest illegal blackjack and poker games in the city. In that capacity, I met and became friends with many of the greats in the entertainment industry, as well as famous sports figures. I had contact with a number of people from the other side of the law too—organized crime. In this book I'll refer to them as "very important people" or "VIPs."

The stories I'll share with you are all true, and in most cases, this may very well be the first time you've heard of them. In those you may have heard of before, such as the 1957 brawl at the Copa involving several New York Yankees players, I'll provide inside details from my position as an eyewitness and participant.

You may find some of my accounts to be serious, humorous, or simply informative. My hope is you will find them all entertaining.

1 : Fisticuffs

One of my early memories is when I graduated from grade school to high school. I was excited because I was in the chorus and we were going to sing on stage during the ceremony. I wasn't much of a cut-up, but I had two friends who were. Before we went on stage, the three of us were talking. Our music teacher told us to quiet down or we'd be excluded from singing. I became very quiet, but not my buddies.

The teacher said to me, "You're out of the exercise."

"Why? I didn't do anything."

"Okay, tell me who did."

I wouldn't give up my friends, and when the chorus was called on stage, I had to stay in my seat. *I was crushed.*

My mother and aunt were in the audience. When the diplomas were handed out and my name was called, they saw me walk up from the student section all by myself and join my classmates. On the way home, my mother asked me about it. I said, "Mama, I got a very special award and they wanted me to walk up there by myself, so I'd get full recognition."

She accepted that explanation and was proud of me.

I went on to Newtown High School in Elmhurst, Queens, where I met the girl who would become my wife a few years later. But my first day there started out with a problem. A kid I didn't know came up to me and said, "Are you Joe Silvestri?"

"Yeah, I am."

"When your older brother went to school here, he beat up my brother. Now I'm gonna kick your ass."

We went to an empty lot across the street from the school to duke it out. There was a big crowd of students around and most of them were rooting for me. I gave that kid a real whipping.

Teaching a bully a lesson was one thing, but I had trouble controlling when and on whom I used my fists. It was an issue that stayed with me most of my life.

* * *

When I turned seventeen in 1949, I quit school and joined the air force. It had just separated from the army and become its own branch. That was one of the biggest blunders I ever made in my life. I didn't know what real racial prejudice was until then.

I went for basic training in Texas, and then on to an assignment in Biloxi, Mississippi. My first problem in Biloxi came when I loaned a black kid in my outfit a civilian sweater I had. He told somebody where he got the sweater and about six guys converged on me in the barracks. They kept saying, "Where is that nigger lover?" They beat the hell out of me with their hands and feet. I sustained some injuries and still have stomach issues after all these years. Following that incident, I became rebellious—the air force wasn't for me and I wanted out.

One day when I was assigned to the company headquarters (HQ), the first sergeant gave me a letter to deliver to another HQ. On my way, I stopped by the field where the football team was practicing and didn't get the letter delivered until about an hour later. When I got back, my first sergeant was pissed off. "Where in the fuck have you been?"

"I got lost. I'd never been there before and couldn't find the right building."

"You lying guinea bastard!"

That was it. I hit him in the face so hard that his eyeglasses became embedded in the bridge of his nose. A bunch of guys grabbed me and took me to my barracks, and then to the stockade. I asked to see a priest and explained the situation to him. He was sympathetic and when I went to my court martial, I was given a general discharge under honorable conditions. I was out of the air force!

They gave me a ride into Biloxi in a Jeep. I was in the back with two MPs, and the first sergeant I'd hit was in the front. He turned to me and said, "If you ever come back on this base, I'll kill you!"

I said, "And if you ever come into town, *I'll* kill *you*."

We never saw each other again.

* * *

I liked Biloxi and stayed there for a while. I got involved with a woman several years older than me named Blossom. She taught me a lot about many things, including sex.

Next, I got a job at the Ballerina Club, which was no small thing being only seventeen. It was kind of like hitting the lottery would be today. What I didn't know at the time was that Blossom was related to the blackjack dealer there—a guy named Murphy. He'd taken a liking to me and she put in a good word for me, so he took me on.

After I was hired, Murphy started training me to deal blackjack. The first thing he did was take the ring off his pinky finger and hand it to me. "If you're going to deal blackjack, you can't have a naked hand. Wearing a ring will make you look more professional," he said. Murphy taught me a lot and he did it in a hurry. Before long, I was ready to go on my own. I broke in on quiet nights and afternoons.

One afternoon when it was really slow, I was playing solitaire when I heard a voice say, "Hey there, Joe Silvestri." I looked up and there was a kid in an air force uniform I knew from Corona. His name was Anthony. I got up from the table and we shook hands and embraced. He said he couldn't wait to get home on leave and tell all the guys that he'd seen me dealing blackjack in a big club. That gave me a real good feeling.

In addition to gambling, the Ballerina had a restaurant and dance hall with live music. They had a quartet with drums, bass, piano, and sax. They were all black and boy, could they wail. Sometimes, when it wasn't busy, I'd listen to them and dance with some of the beautiful women that hung around the club.

One night I met two gorgeous southern belles who looked like twins but weren't even related. I hooked up with one of them and we started seeing each other. It was great for a while, but then Blossom found out. I never knew what a southern temper was like until she went off on me. It was a living hell for a few days, but we got over it and I didn't stray any more.

* * *

One of the guys in the club with whom I became good friends was named Big Pete. He was over six feet tall and weighed around 230 pounds. He was a moose of a man. He was known as the toughest guy in town and nobody messed with him.

I only saw Pete in action one time. We were in the pool room playing a game when a couple of Air Force guys came in with a few drinks under their belts. One of them challenged us to a game. Pete said we weren't interested. The smaller guy said, "What's the matter? Are you afraid we'll kick your ass?"

Pete said, "Take a walk."

Then the bigger guy got right in Pete's face. Pete hit him in the face with that huge right hand of his and knocked him across the floor and into the jukebox. He slammed into it so hard, several of the 45rpm records fell out of their spindles. Pete then kicked the smaller guy in the ass and threw him out the door. We beat it out of there before the MPs showed up.

Another time, Pete, his girlfriend, Blossom, and I went out to dinner in a neighboring town. Over dinner, I had only a couple of drinks, but Pete and his girl downed a lot of booze. When it was time to leave, I offered to drive but Pete refused. He got us back to Biloxi okay, then he turned the wrong way on a one-way street, pulled over, shut the car off, and started smooching it up with his girl.

It wasn't long before a police patrol car pulled up. The two cops got out and one went to each side of the car. It seemed the cop on the driver's side recognized Pete's car, but the cop on the other side pulled his gun out of its holster. The first cop tapped on Pete's window, but with the engine off, the power window wouldn't work and Pete couldn't open it.

I opened my door and asked the cop what he wanted. He said, "I just wanted to know if Pete's car broke down and he needs some help."

At that point, Pete got out of the car, and the cop with his gun drawn came around to the driver's side. The first cop told him, "Put your gun away. *Now.*" The gun went back in its holster.

Pete assured the cops he wasn't having any problems. Everything was fine and he didn't need any help. They got back in their car and drove away. I couldn't believe it. No arrest for driving drunk, not even a ticket for going the wrong way on a one-way street.

Like I said: in Biloxi, nobody messed around with Big Pete.

* * *

http://wbp.bz/afba

CHAPTER 1

SWAT Officer Shot

Denise Gianninoto was a young 32-year-old woman who was living a happy life. She had a good job, owned her own home, had strong family values, and was dating a man, Emit Rice aged 35, who made her feel special. She was aware Emit had made some mistakes earlier in life, one of which was a burglary conviction which made him a convicted felon, but the man she knew seemed to have learned from these mistakes and had changed. She knew he had been previously married and had a six-year-old daughter but Emit's ex-wife and daughter lived in Arizona so he saw very little of his daughter. He had a strong work ethic and was employed as a union carpenter, which paid well. After nearly a year of dating, Denise decided in September, 2000 to take their relationship to the next level and asked Emit to move in with her.

Denise's home was located in the 3700 block of South Torrey Pines, near the area of West Flamingo and Rainbow, in southwest Las Vegas. It was a nice two-story residence with several bedrooms, offering them room to grow. But soon after Emit moved in, she began to see another side of him that made her concerned.

Denise discovered Emit owned a Smith & Wesson 9mm semi-automatic pistol. He had shared with her that he was a convicted felon so Denise knew he was not allowed to possess a firearm. When she confronted him about it, he admitted he knew he wasn't allowed to own one but said he needed a gun for protection. Denise explained she already owned a Colt .380 semi-auto pistol and believed one gun in the house would be sufficient. Emit would get angry and not want to discuss the firearm issue anymore.

In addition to Emit's gun, Denise made another discovery which caused her even more concern. Although Emit had never exhibited it prior to moving in, soon after they began to live together Emit became very possessive over her. At first his possessiveness seemed almost romantic but it increased to alarming levels. He would question her whereabouts and constantly call her at work to see what she was doing and especially check to see if she was meeting with anyone. Denise confronted Emit several times about this and it would escalate into loud arguments. It became so bad that Denise even discussed ending their relationship, which only created further arguments that ended in Emit apologizing and Denise conceding and agreeing to continue trying.

Unfortunately, bad grew to worse. Emit started coming home and drinking every day after work. He would drink beer from the time he came home until he went to bed. His drinking became another source of arguments between the two. Then, in January 2001, Emit was laid off from his union worker job. This caused him to enter a state of depression which only made the drinking worse. Denise explained the arguments between them increased, as did her desire to end the relationship. Emit promised to seek help, eventually seeing a doctor who prescribed him Paxil to aid with his depression.

Denise said she did her best to remain supportive of Emit, but his possessiveness, moodiness, and drinking continued to the point that she needed help. In February, 2001, she called her cousin, 29 year old Marissa Velenta, and asked her to move in with them. Denise used Marissa as someone she could vent to and ask advice. Marissa's presence seemed to only further aggravate Emit as he believed Marissa had moved in to try and split Denise and him apart. He began to argue with Marissa, blaming her for his relationship problems with Denise. Denise would have to intervene, making Emit feel his girlfriend would always take her cousin's side, which would only add to the stress.

In mid-March, 2001, the tension between Emit versus Denise and Marissa became so intense that during an argument with Denise over Emit's mistreatment of Marissa, Denise fled from her own home, fearing Emit would hurt her. Emit chased after Denise, catching her in a neighbor's front yard and knocked her to the ground. Other than the initial knock down, Emit did not punch or strike her. He just pinned Denise to the ground to allow him to finish yelling and making his point, something he did not see any harm in. After eight months of living together, Denise realized their relationship had crumbled past the point of repair and sought Marissa's advice on how she could end it. Little did Denise know that the relationship would deteriorate even further and much sooner than she anticipated.

On April 6, 2001, at approximately 9:30 p.m., Denise and Marissa were at the house, each enjoying a glass of wine on the back patio while waiting for the kitchen floor, which they had just mopped, to finish drying. Emit had gone out earlier in the evening for a night of drinking. When he returned home and walked inside, he was carrying a six pack of beer and found Denise and Marissa out back enjoying their evening. Emit went out back and an argument immediately ensued between him and the two women.

Emit turned his attention towards Marissa, again blaming her for his problems with Denise. His tone grew more intense, adding profane language directed at the younger cousin. Denise had heard enough and intervened, insisting Emit leave the house. Upon being ordered out of the home, Emit became violent and Denise was frightened. She yelled for Marissa to call 911 for help then tried to run away.

Marissa took the cordless telephone and ran into the backyard to call 911. Emit pursued Denise, catching her before she was able to flee the home. He dragged her back into the living room area and retrieved his Smith and Wesson 9mm pistol from the sofa but Denise was able to break free. She ran from the house to the next-door neighbor's home seeking refuge. Emit, chasing her with a pistol in one hand and the six pack of beer he had originally walked into the home with, caught Denise in the neighbor's front yard. He grabbed her by the hair, dragged her across the yard, then back into their own garage, still somehow holding onto both the gun and the beer.

As Marissa was on the phone with the 911 dispatcher, still hiding in the backyard, she was unaware that Emit had retrieved his pistol. She also did not know the two had run from the residence, that Emit had caught Denise, and that he was in the process of dragging her back to the garage. The dispatcher took the information Marissa supplied and the event was dispatched as a violent family disturbance. A patrol sergeant, with nearly 30 years of experience, was nearby when the call was dispatched and arrived only minutes after the call was dispatched.

As the patrol sergeant arrived he saw both Emit and Denise in the garage area. He could see Emit was holding on to Denise but did not see the gun. The sergeant, although not using the soundest tactical approach, pulled his marked patrol car into the driveway of the home and using his public address (PA) system, ordered the couple to exit the garage and walk over to his car. When Emit heard the order, he showed the sergeant his middle finger and closed the garage door as additional patrol cars began to arrive.

The patrol sergeant, upset over Emit's blatant disrespect of authority, ordered the dispatcher to recall the residence and instruct the couple to exit the home. The dispatcher complied with his request and recalled the phone number which had been used to call 911. When the phone rang, Marissa, who was still hiding in the backyard, chose not to answer which allowed Emit to answer. The dispatcher, as instructed, told Emit to exit the home. Emit was incensed and yelled to the police dispatcher that he had a gun, which the dispatcher promptly updated over the radio. The seasoned police sergeant, upon hearing the update, asked the police dispatcher to relay to Emit that the police had guns as well and to again order the occupants out. Emit could hear this radio broadcast over the telephone and informed the dispatcher with the game-changing update; he also had a hostage.

Officers went into the backyard and rescued Marissa where she had been hiding. Upon hearing the officers in the backyard, Emit yelled out, "Get the fuck away from here! I've got a gun and a hostage! I got the gun pointed at her fucking chest!"

At 9:53 p.m., after realizing how the incident had rapidly escalated, the patrol sergeant requested SWAT and Crisis Negotiators respond to the scene. While waiting for these assets to arrive, the police dispatcher was again asked to call into the residence. Emit again answered the phone call, warning the dispatcher to have police stay away. He reiterated that he was armed and only referred to Denise as "his hostage". Rather than rely on updates from the dispatcher, another patrol sergeant arrived and telephoned Emit. After a brief conversation between Emit and the second patrol sergeant, the telephone went dead. Future calls into the residence showed the phone number being out of service and no one knew why.

At approximately 10:14 p.m., just 21 minutes after their request, SWAT and Crisis Negotiators began to arrive. The first few arriving SWAT officers were ordered to "crisis dress" by their SWAT sergeant, who had arrived with them.

When SWAT officers arrive on an incident, they methodically don all of their protective equipment and receive deployment instructions. During a "crisis dress," the first few arriving officers grab just the bare essentials; a ballistic helmet and vest, along with their rifle, then deploy. After other team members arrive, these initial SWAT officers can go back and put on their remaining equipment. The "crisis dress" is typically used only on a confirmed hostage incident and is done should an emergency entry be necessary. Having the first few SWAT officers equipped with the sheer basics allows for an immediate entry should the hostage suddenly be in a life-threatening situation; on the verge of being killed.

As negotiators began to arrive and obtained the briefing on the incident, the SWAT sergeant and four SWAT officers had "crisis dressed" and found the rear sliding glass door would be their immediate entry point until additional team members arrived and other primary entry points were considered.

During the negotiator briefing we learned the Crisis Negotiation Team Leader had been monitoring the event over the police radio and knew it had developed into a confirmed hostage incident. He contacted the local phone company and requested Emit's home telephone line be taken down, to prevent Emit from calling anyone or allowing for friends/family/media from calling in to him. While cell phones existed in 2001, they were not nearly as prevalent as they are today and while unknown to us at that time, neither Emit nor Denise had one.

Our team protocol dictated action by team members should only occur after arrival on scene, briefed on the situation, and authorized by the SWAT Commander. The reasons for this mandate are obvious. While the Team Leader had the best of intentions, it disrupted the conversation the on-scene sergeant was having with Emit.

While acknowledging this mistake, the relationship with the local phone company cannot be overstated. Without the phone companies' assistance, the suspect has the ability to make whatever outgoing calls he chooses from a traditional landline telephone. Should he be talking to someone else, negotiators have no way of talking to him, other than the "beep" indicating an incoming call should the suspect's phone be equipped with a "call-waiting" option.

By having a local phone company representative, ideally one who responds to the scene, negotiators can have the suspect's phone line taken down and a new phone number issued which only the negotiators have access to. Additionally, the suspect's phone can be set up so when he picks up his phone, the negotiator phone rings; he can't make any other outbound calls, forcing him to talk to negotiators. This is only if he does not have a cell phone. Should the suspect have a home phone and cell phone, negotiators have options available which include contacting the cell phone carrier and having the suspect's cell phone service suspended, forcing him to use the home phone. These are options and relationships which negotiation teams should explore prior to an event occurring.

Back at the negotiator briefing, intelligence on the incident was being developed, negotiator assignments were being made, and the phone company was being contacted to expedite restoring Emit's phone service. Just then, the unexpected occurred. Several gunshots were heard emanating from inside Denise's residence.

The SWAT sergeant on-scene, fearing the gunfire was Emit murdering Denise, ordered a "crisis entry". One SWAT officer smashed the rear sliding glass door and the four SWAT officers, along with the SWAT sergeant, made entry into the downstairs living room area. The SWAT officers quickly cleared the downstairs, trying to locate where the gunfire had come from. The lead SWAT officer, Officer Mark Fowler, not finding the suspect downstairs, quickly moved to the staircase area and prepared to ascend upstairs.

SWAT Officer Fowler posted on the staircase, waiting as his partner, SWAT Officer Robert "Jess" Kegley, was coming up from behind to join him. Emit suddenly emerged at the top of the staircase and began firing down towards the officers. One of Emit's initial 9mm rounds found its mark, striking Officer Fowler's left femur. The bullet's impact was so violent, it shattered the femur and caused Officer Fowler's left foot to rotate 180 degrees, pointing towards the rear. As Officer Fowler began to fall, he fired four rounds from his Hecker and Koch, MP-5 Sub Machine Gun while simultaneously yelling out that he had been hit by the suspect's gunfire.

Officer Fowler's partner, Officer Kegley, arrived during the firefight and saw Emit on the landing at the top of the stairs. He brought his MP-5 up and began to fire at Emit but his first round missed and his weapon then jammed. He quickly transitioned to his handgun but as he brought the pistol up, Emit had disappeared from the landing.

While two SWAT officers held their position, covering the staircase from the ground floor, two others conducted a "downed officer rescue" and extracted Officer Fowler from the residence where he was transported to the hospital for emergency care.

Emit had retreated from the staircase landing area into a bedroom where he held Denise. Obviously pumped up and full of adrenaline from the gunfight, Emit yelled down to the SWAT officers, "Fuck you! Come up here and shoot me motherfucker! I got the gun pointed at her chest. I'll kill the bitch!" Even though Denise remained a hostage, after being involved in a gunfight and having a fellow officer shot, it was reported the SWAT officers yelled back some choice statements of their own.

While the phone representative was attempting to reconnect Emit's home phone telephone, communication efforts were turned over to the crisis negotiation team.

From a negotiator's perspective:

By definition, this incident was not a true hostage situation, however that did not matter to Denise. A hostage situation consists of a person being held against their will, being used by the suspect to fulfill a demand. This situation with Emit and Denise is often referred to as a "pseudo-hostage" as it lacks a demand from the suspect. The suspect didn't "take" this person in order to have a commitment fulfilled. "Pseudo-hostage" situations are usually domestic related and highly volatile. The suspect needs nothing from police, except often times wanting the police to leave. These events are of high risk of homicide followed by a suicide. It's embodies the old saying, "If I can't have you, no one will."

As imagined, the scene was chaotic. A woman was being held hostage, a gunfight had occurred, a SWAT officer had been shot, and the only source of communication had been severed.

While waiting for the telephone service to be restored, we had a negotiator go forward with SWAT officers in an armored vehicle to attempt communication over the armored vehicle's PA system.

Sergeant Mike Bunker, the most senior negotiator on the team at the time, was chosen as the primary negotiator, due to his experience. I was assigned to coordinate all of the intelligence on the incident and later filled in as the secondary negotiator.

As SWAT officers were filling in and beefing up their foothold on the bottom floor of the residence and in outer containment positions, the forward negotiator was asked to begin to try and contact Emit using the PA system. Emit could hear some of what the forward negotiator was broadcasting over the PA and SWAT officers inside the residence relayed some of the responses Emit yelled back. Interestingly, Emit specifically asked for a "throw-phone", not a commonly known item in 2001.

After what seemed like an eternity of Emit not having phone service, the phone company was finally able to reestablish the residential connection, yet block it from making any outbound calls. Mike made his first phone call into the home at 11:05 p.m. and spoke to Emit. Unfortunately, the introduction did not go well.

When Emit answered the phone, he was understandably hostile, taking out his frustrations on Mike for the home phone not working. Mike tried to explain to Emit how he had just arrived at the scene but Emit seemed intent on directing his anger at someone and Mike proved a convenient target. As he did his best to calm Emit down, Emit revealed part of his dark plans; he was upset over the house phone not previously working as he said he wanted to call his six year old daughter in Arizona and say goodbye. This showed Emit's intent on committing suicide but he made no mention of Denise, leaving us all to wonder if he had determined her fate as well. As Mike struggled to maintain a dialog over Emit's rants, Emit began to swear at Mike then slammed down the phone.

After a quick group think of possible different approaches and objections we may encounter, Mike called back a few minutes later. The phone rang incessantly until it was finally answered, this time by Denise. She was surprisingly calm. She spoke for less than fifteen seconds before Emit took the phone from her hands and took over the phone conversations. He continued to lash out at Mike, using profanities directed specifically at him, claiming he was talking down to him. When Mike attempted to apologize and continue the conversation, Emit again hung up the phone.

Emit would repeat this type of behavior, answering the phone and swearing at Mike before hanging up, for the next several phone calls. Before ending each call, Emit would scream at him, still accusing him of talking down to him. In hindsight, it would have been a better option to replace the primary negotiator at that point, even if Mike wasn't talking down to Emit, as in the end, all that matters is Emit's perception and we had an innocent third party life on the line. Instead of replacing Mike, the team leader believed since it was early in the negotiation, Emit was just releasing some of his frustration and was using Mike as the outlet, so decided we would press on.

At 11:19 p.m., Emit answered Mike's phone call and provided a chilling warning. Although still irate towards Mike, Emit made it clear that if the police tried to come up the stairs, he would "kill the hostage", choosing the word "hostage" instead of Denise. He further reiterated he wanted to call his daughter to say goodbye. Depersonalizing his girlfriend by referring to her only as "the hostage" and wanting to say goodbye to his daughter were obvious bad signs.

After again being hung up on, Mike again called back into the home and for the first time, Emit expressed his anger towards someone other than Mike. Emit began to explain his hatred toward Denise's cousin, Marissa, and believed the problems he was having with his girlfriend were due to Marissa meddling in their relationship. Just as it appeared Emit would keep his ire directed towards Marissa, Emit again took issue with how Mike was talking to him, causing him yet again to hang up the phone.

After hanging up at 11:30 p.m., Emit refused to answer subsequent phone calls from Mike, forcing them to be picked up by the answering machine. The SWAT officers inside the house could hear the upstairs telephone ringing so knew Emit could hear the phone, he was just choosing not to answer it. On a domestic situation like this, not keeping Emit on the phone, keeping him occupied but also trying to find a peaceful resolution, is dangerous.

We were only twenty-five minutes into Mike trying to talk with Emit and Emit was now refusing to answer the phone. The forward negotiator in the armored vehicle was asked to again try to contact Emit over the PA. For fifteen minutes, Mike called into the residence, only to be greeted by the answering machine while the forward negotiator continued speaking over the PA.

Speaking over the PA gets frustrating as there is often times no response and it's easy to run out of things to say. One of the phrases often used when trying to contact a barricaded subject over the PA is to ask the subject to flip a light on and off so we at least know they can hear us. This sometimes works on a barricaded person who we had yet to make contact with. This phrase is not advisable to use in this situation when Emit is angry, has already spoken with us, and appears to simply not want to talk. Unfortunately, that was the phrase used. Over and over again. "Emit, if you can hear me, please turn the light on or off so we know you're ok". Having that continually repeated, at high decibels, would be irritating.

Emit finally answered the phone at 11:45 p.m., and he was understandably upset about being asked to turn the light on and off whilst the phone continually rang. To make matters worse, as Mike talked to Emit, no one told the forward negotiator we had established phone contact so the broadcast over the PA about turning the lights on and off continued. The left hand didn't know what the right was doing. We looked like buffoons and Emit made sure to tell Mike this, of course using stronger terminology, before hanging up again.

The subsequent telephone call into the residence was answered by Denise. All she was able to say was that she was ok and Emit again took the phone from her. As he was berating Mike for how he felt he was being talked to, he explained that he simply wanted twenty minutes to try and think things over. Considering his early statements about wanting to say goodbye to his daughter and his current irate condition, agreeing to a long period of "no-contact" is risky and Mike knew it. Mike had Emit agree to a fifteen minute break before hanging up at midnight.

Everyone in the command post held their breath for fifteen minutes, hoping things would remain quiet during that time frame and not have the silence shattered by gunfire, given Emit's earlier statements and the known risk for homicide/ suicide. It became even more concerning when Emit broke his promise and refused to answer Mike's phone call at 12:15 a.m..

At 12:20 a.m., Emit finally answered Mike's phone call. It didn't go unnoticed that he answered at the twenty minute mark, like he had originally asked for. When Emit did answer, his demeanor was much calmer and he actually thanked Mike for allowing him to have the break. But of course he wanted more. He explained to Mike he was in the process of trying to work out some issues with his girlfriend and wanted five more minutes. Probably because this was the first time he was spoken kindly to, and possibly because he viewed Emit's reference to speaking to his "girlfriend" and not "hostage" as a sign of progress, Mike agreed to the additional five minutes.

At 12:25 a.m., Emit answered Mike's scheduled phone call. He remained thankful for the time Mike allotted to him and said he was still working things out with Denise, actually using her first name. This all was viewed as positive. Emit then relayed what was believed to be one of the core issues causing his irrational behavior; he shared he was fearful of the adjudication coming from his pending court case.

All eyes were suddenly on me. I had been responsible for providing all of Emit's background information. I had checked his local arrests, national arrests, (through N.C.I.C.), driver's license queries, pawn records, marriage information, and anything else I could think of. I learned about and shared the details to his earlier Burglary conviction but I wasn't aware of anything new as there were no arrests listed. Emit had also not mentioned anything earlier during any of our conversations with him. But because of this statement, I knew I missed something.

I quickly accessed the police computer system and logged into the court records to view upcoming cases. It was there I made a startling discovery. Emit had been served an indictment on two felony charges; Sexual Assault on a Minor Under 14 Years of Age and Lewdness with a Minor Under 14 Years of Age. The victim was his step-daughter from his previous marriage. My heart sank.

The court records program listed the prosecutor assigned to the case and even though it was after midnight, I was able to get the prosecutor's home phone number and called her.

She explained to me the horrid details of the case and said she had recently been in contact with Emit and his attorney where they had negotiated a plea agreement. While the plea agreement had yet to be accepted by the judge, because of the details to the crimes he committed with his step-daughter and considering his ex-felon status, the prosecutor explained how Emit had agreed to accept a prison sentence of nearly twenty years. He was expected to surrender to 'walk-through' arrest the following week and would proceed to the sentencing after his plea.

Although Emit had not been arrested for these charges, hence not showing in his arrest record as the charges were initiated through an indictment, there was no excuse for me not initially checking court records for pending cases as these would have shown up. I quickly, and sheepishly, went back and shared with the SWAT Commander, Negotiation Team Leader, and other negotiators the information I had confirmed. This information was also passed along to Mike.

After two hours of negotiations, the relationship between Emit and Mike was still challenging; Mike tried to establish rapport and dialog but Emit would remain irate, believing Mike was condescending. Even though Mike was not the one who had continually harped over the PA system about turning the lights on and off and was not the person who failed to get the needed intelligence which would help develop themes to deal with Emit's issues, a change in the primary negotiator was long overdue.

Detective Michael Eylar, who had been serving as the secondary negotiator for Mike, was the natural choice to assume the role of primary negotiator, as he had already listened to the entire previous conversation. I was placed as Michael's secondary.

At 12:54 a.m., Michael placed his first call into Emit. Emit was confused at first, wanting to know what happened to Mike and asked to speak with him. But as Michael continued to talk, Emit seemed more accepting and didn't hang up the phone, which was a marked improvement.

Michael's approach and tone of voice appeared to work. Emit became more rational and just five minutes into their conversation he offered our first glimmer of hope; Emit said he planned on letting Denise come out. Although he didn't specify when he planned on releasing her, the fact that Emit brought this up was the most positive sign to occur since we began the event.

Emit remained comfortable with Michael, expounding on his concerns of the pending court case and the prison time he knew he would have to serve. Although we were happy Emit continued to talk, didn't appear as angry, and hadn't hung up on Michael, we did ask Michael to gently nudge Emit on when he planned on releasing Denise. Emit was very straightforward when asked, explaining Denise would come out in one hour. He continued his straightforwardness, explaining he would kill himself after Denise exited.

Michael took the opportunity to conduct suicide intervention; explaining how suicide is a permanent solution to a temporary problem. He agreed that serving the prison time would suck but explained that even though he may be locked up, he would still have many people who would care for him and he could still correspond with. Emit would not agree with Michael, just reiterating he would let Denise free but did intend to follow through with killing himself after her release.

At 1:09 a.m., just fifteen minutes after Michael had begun talking with him, Emit said he was going to send Denise downstairs to the waiting SWAT officers. This seemed odd as he had just explained it would be an hour. Emit said he would have to hang up the telephone so he could say his goodbyes to her as he acknowledged it would be the last time he would ever see her. Although this was risky, Michael agreed, knowing Emit was going to hang up if he wanted to anyway and agreeing to it allowed the rapport to build.

We did advise the SWAT Commander of the possibilities of homicide/suicide when Emit hung up which the commander broadcast to the SWAT officers.

After a tense four minutes, Michael called back and Emit answered, announcing Denise would be walking downstairs. Michael thanked him for this and the SWAT Commander briefed the SWAT officers positioned on the ground floor to expect her presence. Several minutes passed but Denise never appeared. Fearful, Michael placed several phone calls to the residence but each time the phone was picked up then promptly disconnected. We were all on pins and needles, wondering what was going on and how much we should push with repeated phone calls.

At 1:18 a.m., Emit answered the phone and again claimed Denise was exiting. Michael spoke to Emit for two long minutes when suddenly an upstairs door opened and Denise walked downstairs and into the arms of a waiting SWAT officer. Three and a half hours of having a gun trained on her, threatened with death by the man she had loved, Denise was finally safe.

After she was removed from the inner perimeter, we had the opportunity to debrief her, hoping she could provide us with something we could use to change Emit's mind on his intent to take his own life. Denise was obviously overwhelmed but said she believed Emit remained intent on fulfilling his desire. She cautioned us that in addition to the Smith and Wesson 9mm pistol he owned, Emit also had what she believed were one hundred rounds of ammunition for the pistol and two spare magazines. She also explained he was in possession of her Colt .380 semi-automatic pistol. This information was shared with the SWAT Commander who promptly briefed his SWAT officers.

We asked Denise about the delay when Emit first said she was coming out until she finally came out twelve minutes later. She explained when Emit first told her she could leave, she was free to do so but she was scared. We assumed she meant she was afraid for Emit, scared he would hurt himself when she left. Denise was quick to correct us. She said she was extremely afraid that when she started to walk out, she felt Emit would shoot her in the back. She said it took her the twelve minutes to work up the courage to walk out and finally just took her chances that Emit wouldn't shoot.

Michael had stayed on the telephone with Emit as Denise came down the stairs to the awaiting SWAT officers. While she was taken to a safe location, Michael praised Emit for doing the right thing. He then switched gears, trying to convince Emit that better days still lay ahead and asked him to come out and meet with him personally. Emit refused the meet offer, explaining he would not come out. He then shared the same information Denise had just relayed; that he had one hundred bullets and two magazines, implying he was ready for a shootout should police try to assault him. When Michael tried to reassure him that no one would come up the stairs, Emit said he didn't trust Michael and hung up the phone. This was the first time Emit treated Michael poorly.

At 1:28 a.m., two and a half hours after negotiators first spoke with Emit, Michael called back into the house and again talked to him. Emit became very stoic, explaining he was tired of playing games with us and he was going to follow through with his plan and kill himself. Michael tried to intervene, but Emit made one final eerie remark claiming, "It's been fun", then hung up the phone.

Michael could hear the finality in Emit's voice and redialed his number. Michael made several calls to the home but each one went unanswered. Finally, at 1:38 a.m., only eight minutes after ending his last phone call, SWAT officers downstairs reported hearing one shot coming from the upstairs area of the home. We all knew what that meant.

The SWAT Commander still had to go through the motions. Although Emit wouldn't answer the phone after saying he was going to kill himself and a single gunshot was heard, this was the same person who had open fired on several SWAT officers, striking one of them. He was still upstairs, in an elevated position of advantage, so they had to make sure Emit was not simply playing possum.

SWAT officers inserted a listening device but nothing could be heard. They deployed several gas rounds but still no movement or sounds were detected. At 2:16 a.m., SWAT officers were authorized to ascend the stairs which began the slow methodical search task. At 2:31 a.m., nearly five hours after the incident first began, SWAT officers on the second floor of the residence broadcasted they had located Emit deceased in the upstairs bathroom area from a self-inflicted gunshot wound to the head.

Although we as negotiators made several mistakes on this event, we were able to walk away from it with a partial win; Denise's safe release. I'm not certain that even had we played our cards perfectly on this event and developed a strong initial rapport with Emit, we would have been successful in having him exit and taken into custody without incident. I think Emit knew that in addition to committing the heinous sexual acts on his minor step-daughter, following it up with shooting a SWAT officer sealed his fate of knowing he would never be a free man. However, even with everything Emit had done wrong, we still did everything we could to get him out safe.

Lessons Learned:

We were very fortunate there were no additional police officers injured in this event as we put ourselves in a poor position from the start of the event. Police officers are taught during the first portion of the academy the importance of using good tactics when arriving on calls. We are also taught that family disturbances can be some of the most dangerous calls police officers respond to. When arriving on a call, police officers are taught to park several houses away from the incident and to approach the location, with their partner, in a way that provides them some cover yet still allows them to see and hear what is going on. They are certainly never taught to drive directly into the driveway of the residence!

No one ever asked the 30-year sergeant why he pulled directly into the driveway. No one asked why he chose to use the PA radio versus exiting his patrol car and give verbal commands to have Emit and Denise exit the garage. In this incident, we are probably very lucky the sergeant did not open his patrol car door to confront them as the sergeant did not see Emit armed with the pistol and Emit certainly would have had the drop on the sergeant.

When the dispatcher was told to call into the residence and was told by Emit that he was armed with a gun, it was not a wise choice for the sergeant to relay back that the police were outside and had guns too. Even though when officers first arrived they were unaware it was a hostage incident, trying to exert authority, and using a third party to do, (the dispatcher), will likely never produce positive results.

A second sergeant showed up on scene and was able to make telephone contact with Emit. As discussed, when the Crisis Negotiation Team Leader was enroute to the location, he contacted the phone company to have Emit's telephone line taken down. During these type of critical events, best case practice is to isolate the suspect's phone line, forcing him to only speak with the negotiator. But there are certainly a lot of "what if's" and every scenario is different. Just as this incident showed, a police supervisor had telephone contact with Emit. What if they had tremendous rapport? Is there any reason to shut down the phone line? Unless the suspect is doing something that shows a true need for the phone to be disrupted, these types of decisions should only be made at the scene.

Whenever the police first make contact with a suspect on these types of events, it is exceptionally normal for the suspect to lash out at the officer and make spiteful comments. As the event goes on, this anger normally subsides and a regular conversation can be had. Emit lashed out at Mike when their phone conversation began but Emit never returned to normal. It was clear there was a personality conflict between Emit and Mike as Emit believed he was being talked down to. Although none of us listening felt that way, the only person's opinion who matters was Emit's, as he was holding a hostage. We certainly did not want to further aggravate him. Looking back, we should have switched negotiators much sooner than we did. When we finally did switch and put Michael on as the primary negotiator, we saw a huge positive change in Emit's demeanor.

Some of Emit's anger towards Mike was due to voice commands he was receiving over the PA system, especially while he was on the phone with Mike. This was simply poor communications between the negotiators, not being clear with the negotiator announcing over the PA radio, on when to start and stop talking. It was also not helpful to simply repeat the commands of turning the house light on and off, over and over again. That would make anyone inside a house irritated. The negotiator who was operating the PA was new and was not sure what he should say. The team leader should have made sure the new negotiator was properly prepared before sending him to broadcast verbal instructions over the PA radio.

The failure to check pending court cases was huge. Had I done this check at the beginning of the incident, we would have likely known some of the reasons Emit was so adamant about ending the event violently. Emit knew he was going to prison and would be there for a very long time. Had we known that at the beginning, we could have tried to develop strategies to help soften this when it was brought up on the phone. To help prevent making these type of mistakes, we created a template of sources to be checked on all future events. While it might seem basic, it has helped us from making this same mistake twice.

CHAPTER 2

Fremont Street Sniper

For those not familiar with Las Vegas, the location of the city's most famous attractions and gambling areas have changed over time. The current Las Vegas strip, located on Las Vegas Boulevard, is home to some of the world's largest and most glamorous hotels and gaming establishments. However, prior to the 1950s, this "strip" was nonexistent. Las Vegas was still famous for gaming during those times but those establishments were in the heart of Downtown Las Vegas, located on Fremont Street. These older casinos, such as the Four Queens, Golden Nugget and The California, still exist today and the area is currently being revitalized. Less than ten blocks east of downtown, yet still on Fremont Street, lies a series of daily/weekly rentals. These rentals are sometimes frequented by less than law abiding people. Such was the case on January 7, 2003.

On January 7, 2003, at approximately 3:25 a.m., LVMPD dispatch began to receive several 911 calls reporting 7 to 12 gunshots heard coming from an apartment complex located at Fremont Street and 15th Street. As those calls were coming in, the night clerk for the apartment complex was in the front lobby area and witnessed a black male adult run through the lobby area, armed with a rifle, firing shots indiscriminately. The night clerk also called 911 to report the suspect was last seen running out the backdoor of the lobby area, towards the rear alley.

Within two minutes of these calls, several single-man patrol vehicles began arriving in the area of the apartment complex, which consists of multiple three-level apartment buildings. One of the arriving officers pulled into the north alleyway and found a male on the ground with a gunshot wound to the head. As the officer was broadcasting this updated information, two additional single-manned patrol cars began to arrive at the front of the apartment complex, near the lobby area. These two units heard additional gunfire occurring, broadcast the information, and started deploying AR-15 rifles to prepare for an active shooter event. Several of these rounds were suspected of being fired toward the officer arriving in the alley who was checking on the man on the ground.

As the gunfire stalled, the officer in the north alley could see the victim was shot in the head and obviously deceased. As additional gunfire erupted, officers could hear it but did not know where it was coming from. It was emanating from the center of the complex area as the suspect, unbeknownst to the officers, was firing randomly. He made his way on foot through the buildings to apartment building "E", located on the southern end of the complex. It was at this southern building that the suspect went to the third floor, into apartment #307. This studio apartment had one window which faced west towards downtown Las Vegas. The window also provided a view of the apartment complex across the street as well as a vantage of the front of the current apartment complex where additional police vehicles were beginning to arrive.

Undetected in this third-floor apartment, the suspect continued to shoot, firing multiple rifle rounds from the west facing window. He fired multiple rounds at the apartment complex directly south across the street, striking an unsuspecting citizen in the chest who was standing on his balcony. The arriving patrol cars out front also provided for ample targets of opportunity. The suspect continued his rifle fire, hitting one patrol car at least ten times. One of those rounds fired fragmented causing the jagged round to continue on until it found its mark, striking an officer in the leg.

http://wbp.bz/hha

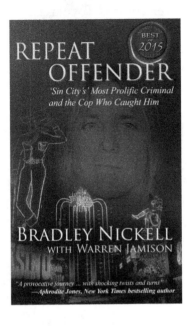
1

In Danger
Just as courage is the danger of life, so is fear its safeguard.
—Leonardo da Vinci

Early one evening, I left the Detective Bureau and soon noticed the same compact car had been in my mirror for a few blocks. A silver colored Toyota, beat-up looking with no front license plate, driven by two Hispanic-looking men. I wasn't sure if they were following me, but I didn't want to take a chance. My nerves were shot. I'd been dreading this exact thing for weeks.

A quick turn down a side street didn't lose them. Maybe if I stopped, they'd pass, but that would've made me an easy drive-by target and I was outnumbered.

I hastily formed my plan. If they continued to follow, I'd phone for patrol units to pull them over as I led them around aimlessly. A call over the police radio might tip them off, though, if they had a scanner.

I hoped a quick jaunt on the freeway might lose them, but they were still there, just a few cars behind, in the lane to my right. The rush-hour traffic slowed. Something ahead was bringing traffic to a complete stop. If these guys were assassins, this might be their best chance—pull up next to me and unload everything they have. The tactic is used south of the border more often than people in the United States know, and they're usually armed to the teeth.

I was ready. One hand on my pistol in my lap and a pump-action 12-gauge shotgun lying across the seat next to me. The car drew up on my right, and I waited for the smallest of signs. The pistol rested between my legs as I jacked a round into the shotgun's chamber. I could feel my pulse beating in my neck.

The driver rolled his window down and threw out a spent cigarette. His chiseled face, backed with dark, lifeless eyes, reminded me of a shark. I pointed the shotgun directly at him, just out of view below the door frame. Safety off. Finger on the trigger.

Each of the five rounds in the shotgun had nine, .33-caliber projectiles inside, just waiting to tear through the door panel and eliminate the threat.

He had no idea what a bad decision he was about to make. Time seemed to stand still.

Neither the driver nor the passenger had even glanced at me. Traffic started to flow again and the moment was over. I relaxed my grip on the shotgun and holstered my pistol. Before I could reflect, I was on the next freeway exit, contemplating another path home.

My heart raced. I had mixed thoughts: thankful it turned out to be nothing, and disturbed that Daimon had gotten inside my head.

Police work is rarely as you see on TV. Real investigations don't begin and end in an hour. Some take months, or years, to complete. And heart-racing, adrenaline-filled moments are sometimes scarce in the endless days of the work grind. But every now and then, maybe once in a career for some cops, a case comes along that could've been conceived by a Hollywood screenwriter.

Weeks before, Chief Deputy District Attorney Sandy DiGiacomo had called; her tone urgent. "Brad, detectives just told me someone has put a hit out on me."

My heart began to thud heavily. A contract killing is nothing to take lightly, especially for a prosecutor who has made a lot of daunting enemies.

"They asked me where my kids are, and said I might want to get them from school." Her voice shook. "And you'll never guess who the bad guy is."

"No way," I said, knowing exactly what she meant.

"Yep . . . Daimon Monroe."

Sandy and I had been working an investigation involving Daimon, a thief who had probably committed more crimes than anyone I've ever known. Clearly, things had just taken a turn for the worse.

"You do whatever they say," I said, picturing Daimon. At first blush, he seemed harmless, small in stature, dressed like a rock star from the 80s, walking with a tough swagger to counterbalance his effeminate appearance. But he was a vain and dangerously clever man with dead eyes. I had a sick feeling in my stomach. "I'll see if I can find out more and give you a call."

Daimon had been in jail for months waiting to be tried on several cases, but he still had access to the phone, mail, and a network of friends on the outside. I was the lead detective in his criminal affairs. Sandy was prosecuting him as a habitual criminal, which meant if he were convicted, he potentially faced a life sentence.

As a detective in the Las Vegas Repeat Offender Program, or ROP team, I know a court case against one thief doesn't seem particularly noteworthy. Not until someone realizes the criminal is repeatedly committing crimes, do people start to see the effect one criminal has on a vast amount of innocent people. And Daimon was the most devious, calculating, prolific thief Nevada had ever seen, stealing millions of dollars of material goods, destroying livelihoods, threatening lives, and harming those who stumbled into his path.

Knowing what I did about Daimon, Sandy could be in real danger. I began checking the recorded inmate phones from Daimon's housing unit hoping to find him, or another prisoner, talking about anything that might indicate whether the threat was real or simply jailhouse talk. The inmates know the phones are recorded, and yet many still talk about their criminal activities. Most of them are smart enough to at least use coded language, but some don't bother.

Each phone call lasted around ten minutes and then the line is automatically disconnected. Depending on how many inmates are in a particular housing unit, there can be anywhere from a few dozen to a few hundred phone calls per unit, per day. Sorting through the calls to find a particular inmate's activity was like finding needles in a haystack. And listening to the calls takes time, as you have to remain alert and mentally invested in each conversation or important information can slip by unnoticed.

After hours of searching and listening, one series of phone calls caught my attention.

An inmate named Johnny had called a man named Rich. Johnny had a thick, Hispanic accent and spoke in rough street-language, but Rich sounded more formal, refined, probably educated.

"Hey, listen," Johnny said. "There's a hit out on a D.A. here, named DiGiacomo. I leaked it to some dummy, and he leaked it downstairs, thinking it was gonna get him somewhere. The guy trying to get this done is Diamond Holt or something like that."

One of Daimon's alias last names is Hoyt. Johnny must've seen some paperwork. Diamond Holt...Daimon Hoyt.

In another phone call, Johnny sounded panicked and began to whisper, so he couldn't be heard by other inmates. "Things have changed since we last spoke, man. He still wants the hit on the D.A., but now he's talking about some detective, and a Judge Leavitt, too."

Johnny sounded like he'd gotten into something he wanted no part of. He didn't want to snitch, but he couldn't sit by and let the hits go down. So he leaked it, knowing the guy would pass the tip to the cops.

Johnny said Daimon was trying to find someone to do the hits for $10,000 each. He also said Daimon might've made a connection with the Aryan Warriors prison gang, and they might've farmed it out to the Sureños gang in Southern California.

This wasn't just jailhouse talk. This was for real.

"He says his number one is this detective named Nickell."

"I'm gonna have somebody come see you," Rich said.

I stopped the tape and replayed it. *"His number one is this detective named Nickell."* Leaning back in my chair, I clasped my hands behind my head and exhaled. This was a first. As a cop, I've had people threaten me in highly charged, emotional moments, but nobody had ever hatched a real plot to kill me. I was just a cop, doing my job. Daimon was making it personal. I'd worked hard to put the Monroe investigation to rest, but things were far from over. ◇

2

A Dawning Criminal
Why would we look to the past in order to prepare for the future? Because there is nowhere else to look.
—James Burke

Daimon's adult interactions with law enforcement began fifteen years before his case reached my desk.

In October of 1991, the owner of a high-tech sound equipment business in Las Vegas reported a break in. Oddly, among the items stolen was a pair of two-way radios he used with his employees at his store. He had other shop radios still operating on the same frequency, so when suddenly he began hearing conversations at night between strangers, he suspected the burglars were now using the radios while committing other burglaries.

The Las Vegas police borrowed one of the radios to monitor the traffic.

A couple of quiet nights passed, and then the suspicious radio traffic resumed. The first names Daimon, Bobby, and Chris were casually used over the radio. Daimon was careless enough one night to announce the license plate number for his own pickup truck. From that, the police were able to identify him and figure out where he lived.

After a couple weeks of off-and-on surveillance, officers identified Robert Holmes and Christopher Clayland as

Daimon's associates. Finally, one night, the hard work panned out. Undercover officers watched Daimon and Chris break into a business.

When they were arrested, their apartments were searched and found to be loaded with stolen property from multiple commercial burglaries. The find included artwork, expensive sound equipment, video equipment, televisions, musical instruments, fish tanks, computers, and various other items. Officers also located a storage unit Daimon rented filled with expensive stolen property.

Daimon's girlfriend at the time, Regina Aurelia, as well as Robert Holmes, were also implicated in the crimes and arrested.

The next day, an officer went to the jail to speak with Daimon. He had never been in real trouble before. Daimon confessed to numerous commercial burglaries, providing planning and execution details. He described how, in one burglary, he used socks over his hands because he forgot gloves and didn't want to leave fingerprints. In another burglary, Daimon said he came in from the roof, took expensive sound equipment, and fled through the back door. In several burglaries, he used a screwdriver to jimmy the front door of the business and, once, he used bolt cutters to cut open a semi-trailer behind a K-Mart to steal bedding and boxes of toilet paper.

In the early 1990s, society was still in its infancy of the digital age. The officer didn't have a device with him to record Daimon's confession, but he planned to return the next day. Daimon claimed he would continue to cooperate.

When the officer interviewed Regina, she also said she would cooperate, in order to "get this whole thing over with so I can move on with my life." She confessed her guilt, acknowledged the stolen property in her possession, and said she was aware Daimon had been committing burglaries. The officer said he'd return the following day to record her statement as well.

When the officer returned, Daimon unexpectedly stopped cooperating. He said his attorney told him to say he made up the earlier statements because he was scared. "You won't be able to prove the charges," he said as he laughed. Daimon said he would tell the judge the officer violated his rights and beat him up to make him confess. "It's funny that I told you about all that stuff and you can't prove it because you didn't record me telling you." Daimon refused to say anything else.

The officer contacted Regina again. She'd also spoken with Daimon's attorney. She declined to cooperate further, though she did say she wouldn't recant her earlier confession.

Daimon was found guilty by a jury on eight counts of burglary and seven counts of grand larceny. He was sentenced to twelve years in prison. After the verdicts, he pled guilty to burglary and possession of stolen property in another case and was sentenced to concurrent time with the twelve-year sentence.

Regina also pled guilty to burglary and was sentenced to ten years in prison. Her sentence was suspended, and she was placed on probation for five years. Chris Clayland pled guilty to two counts of burglary and was sentenced to eight years in prison. Robert Holmes pled guilty to one count of attempted burglary. He was sentenced to two years in prison, which was suspended. He was placed on probation for four years.

Daimon served a little over three of the twelve years and was paroled to the streets in 1995. By that time, Regina had her probation transferred to California, and she was out of Daimon's life for good.

Late at night, on August 14, 1995, a citizen saw two men smash a Las Vegas recording studio window and leave— probably testing to see if the business had a burglar alarm. The men returned about thirty minutes later and were seen prying the front door open. The citizen called the police, and officers were dispatched. Arriving officers found two men walking in the parking lot. The officers ordered the men over to their car, but instead, they took off running.

One of the men was caught in the parking lot and identified as Engelbert Clifford. He went by "Engel" for short. The other man—Daimon Monroe—was caught by a K-9 unit nearby. He tried to confuse the police with a fake ID and the name Devon Matthews, but the cops didn't believe him.

Engel said he met Daimon in a bar, where he was promised easy money if he'd be a lookout. They'd come to the recording studio to break in and steal sound equipment, according to Engel.

A couple of days later, the court released Daimon from jail with an appearance date. When he didn't show up for court, a bench warrant was issued. Detectives began looking for him and, before long, found a girlfriend and an address.

June 13, 1996—surveillance began at the girlfriend's address. That very day, Daimon and a pregnant looking, blonde, teenage girl, about sixteen years old, arrived in a pick-up truck. To get a better look, a detective drove past the house. Daimon quickly backed out of the driveway and followed the detective down the street.

When other detectives tried to pull him over, Daimon rammed an undercover police car just as the detective stepped from the vehicle. The impact moved the police car several feet. Luckily, the detective was unharmed. Daimon almost ran over another detective then fled in the truck. The detectives began pursuit.

Daimon took the police on a car chase at breakneck speeds, blowing through stop signs and traffic signals for almost twenty miles on the streets of Las Vegas. He got on the freeway briefly and then tried to exit. On the exit ramp, he lost control. The truck rolled twice, spilling its contents across the road.

The police called an ambulance and when the paramedics had Daimon inside, he asked them to retrieve a black bag that had been thrown from the wreck. Inside the bag, detectives found a semi-automatic pistol. After his release from the hospital, Daimon was booked on his warrant and new charges of felony evading and felon possessing a firearm. He eventually pled guilty to evading and possession, and the burglary of the recording studio was dismissed as part of negotiations. Daimon received a twelve-year, prison sentence consecutive to the time left on his parole. He was now a nineteen-time convicted felon.

Engel had no prior felony convictions. He pled guilty to conspiracy to commit burglary and received nine months in the county jail, which was suspended. He was put on probation.

Daimon discharged from prison at the end of December, 2000. Five days later, and well past midnight, an officer spotted him acting suspiciously in a commercial area. Daimon gave the officer different names, trying to conceal his identity, but the officer figured out who he was from police records. Only then did Daimon tell the officer he'd just gotten out of prison. Daimon went to jail for providing false information and failure to register as a convicted felon, two misdemeanors that resulted in a few days in jail.

On March 17, 2003, at almost one in the morning, a citizen called the police to report two suspicious men outside a motorcycle dealership. The men were seen peering through a window and ducking behind the building. Police officers arrived and quickly found the men wearing dark clothing and gloves, briskly walking away from the building. The officers stopped the men who were found carrying flashlights in their pockets. These men were Daimon and Engel; both gave fake names.

Daimon and Engel said they were looking for cardboard boxes because Engel was planning to move. When asked how they got there, both said they rode the city bus.

One officer asked, "How are you guys going to get a bunch of boxes on the bus when you head back home?"

Daimon became belligerent and told Engel, "Don't tell them anything, don't say a thing."

The cops found Daimon's Chrysler minivan about two-hundred yards away. Inside the van were pry bars, screwdrivers, another flashlight, a Slim Jim, and an array of other tools.

Daimon was arrested for possession of burglary tools, failing to register as an ex-felon, and providing false information to the police. He was eventually sentenced to a short jail sentence and community service. Engel was arrested on outstanding bench warrants.

July 18, 2003—Daimon was stopped with a man named Bryan Fergason after midnight in an alley behind a strip mall. There had been a rash of burglaries in the area, but the officer found no cause to arrest them. He made a record of the contact and documented Bryan as an associate of Daimon's.

A mere thirteen days later, on July 31, 2003, at 1:15 a.m., Daimon and Bryan Fergason were driving around in Daimon's minivan. A citizen reported them as involved in suspicious activity, and the information was broadcast over the police radio. After spotting the minivan, an officer pulled them over. The officer believed they were casing for burglaries, as he found pry bars, two-way radios, gloves, and flashlights in the van. After a short time, the officer let them go without charges, believing he couldn't prove the tools were to be used for committing burglaries.

That was the last time Daimon would have such a simple run-in with the cops. ◇

http://wbp.bz/roa

See even more at:
http://wbp.bz/tc

More True Crime You'll Love From WildBlue Press

A MURDER IN MY HOMETOWN by Rebecca Morris
Nearly 50 years after the murder of seventeen year old Dick Kitchel, Rebecca Morris returned to her hometown to write about how the murder changed a town, a school, and the lives of his friends.

wbp.bz/hometowna

BETRAYAL IN BLUE by Burl Barer & Frank C. Girardot Jr.
Adapted from Ken Eurell's shocking personal memoir, plus hundreds of hours of exclusive interviews with the major players, including former international drug lord, Adam Diaz, and Dori Eurell, revealing the truth behind what you won't see in the hit documentary THE SEVEN FIVE.

wbp.bz/biba

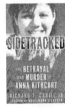

SIDETRACKED by Richard Cahill
A murder investigation is complicated by the entrance of the Reverend Al Sharpton who insists that a racist killer is responsible. Amid a growing media circus, investigators must overcome the outside forces that repeatedly sidetrack their best efforts.

wbp.bz/sidetrackeda

BETTER OFF DEAD by Michael Fleeman
A frustrated, unhappy wife. Her much younger, attentive lover. A husband who degrades and ignores her. The stage is set for a love-triangle murder that shatters family illusions and lays bare a quiet family community's secret world of sex, sin and swinging.

wbp.bz/boda

CPSIA information can be obtained
at www.ICGtesting.com
Printed in the USA
FSHW020731130920
73745FS